backyards for
KIDS

by Ziba Kashef and the Editors of Sunset Books, Menlo Park, California

SUNSET BOOKS

VP, EDITORIAL DIRECTOR
Bob Doyle

DIRECTOR OF SALES
Brad Moses

DIRECTOR OF OPERATIONS
Rosann Sutherland

MARKETING MANAGER
Linda Barker

ART DIRECTOR
Vasken Guiragossian

STAFF FOR THIS BOOK

MANAGING EDITOR
Jennifer Block Martin

SENIOR EDITOR
Ben Marks

DESIGNER
Susan Paris

PHOTO EDITOR
Eligio Hernández

COPY EDITOR
Gail Nelson-Bonebrake

PRODUCTION SPECIALIST
Linda M. Bouchard

PROOFREADER
Elissa Rabellino

INDEXER
Ken DellaPenta

COVER PHOTOGRAPHS Main image, bottom left, and
second-from-bottom left by Michele Lee Willson;
styling by Laura Del Fava. Top left by Bill Bachmann/
Photo Network. Second-from-top left by Lisa
Romerein/Jupiter Images.

For additional copies of *Backyards for Kids* or any
other Sunset book, visit us at www.sunsetbooks.com.

For more exciting home and garden ideas, visit
myhomeideas.com

contents

READERS' NOTE: Almost any do-it-yourself project involves a risk of some sort. Your tools, materials, and skills will vary, as will the conditions at your project site. Sunset Publishing Corporation has made every effort to be complete and accurate in the instructions and other content contained in this publication. However, the publisher does not assume any responsibility or liability for damages or losses sustained or incurred in the course of your project or in the course of your use of it. Always follow manufacturer's operating instructions in the use of tools, check and follow your local building codes, and observe all standard safety precautions.

backyard
basics

A FAMILY-FRIENDLY YARD WELCOMES CHILDREN WITH DESIGNATED PLAY AREAS, AGE-APPROPRIATE STRUCTURES, AND ROOM FOR SPONTANEOUS FUN. IT ALSO LEAVES PLENTY OF SPACE FOR ADULTS. THIS CHAPTER GUIDES YOU THROUGH SUCH PRACTICAL MATTERS AS SITE PLANNING, SAFE PLANTS, BUILDING MATERIALS, TOOLS, AND STORAGE.

GETTING STARTED

YOU'RE READY TO DIVE INTO TRANSFORMING your backyard into the perfect play space for your kids. That could mean a wide-open lawn with lots of room for running and games. Or maybe you're picturing an environment filled with irresistible kid-friendly amenities like a pool, tree house, or play set. Your goals may be guided at first by your yard's size and your children's ages, but don't limit yourself. You might find you can do more to bring the backyard alive than you ever imagined.

Keep in mind, too, that your yard is a dynamic space that will grow and change as your family does. Like a chameleon, it will need to shift and adjust as your children age and their interests develop. It should, of course, also accommodate activities you and your spouse enjoy.

To stay fresh over time, backyard play spaces should encourage multiple activities. In a child's mind, a sandbox is a kitchen for making sand pies one day and a busy construction site the next. And forts can serve both as hide-outs for daydreaming and clubhouses when friends come over.

Kids tend to be more respectful of gardens when they are involved in the planning and planting.

How to Make It Happen

Involve your kids as much as possible in backyard planning. Remember that your job is to provide the stage, not to write the entire script. Once you've settled on some basic plans, choose one of these three strategies:

- BUILD IT. Save money by constructing that rope swing or skateboard ramp yourself, or enlist the help of friends and neighbors. Follow instructions in this book and those that come with any kit to make sure you get the right materials and build safely.
- BUY IT. Shop online or at home-improvement centers for a do-it-yourself kit. With a kit, you can more easily put together complex structures like a playhouse or a swing-and-slide set.
- HIRE A PRO. If you don't have the time or skill to do it yourself, consult a licensed builder or contractor. It's wise to talk to several pros and get their bids before settling on the one to hire.

To keep an eye on your kids, situate a table and a couple of chairs near their play area.

Kids Wish List: An Age-by-Age Guide

1 to 2 Years

- Steps to climb and descend
- Sand, buckets, and shovels
- Wagons to load and pull
- Bucket swing seats that prevent toddlers from falling out
- Short slides, with help from an adult
- Tunnels to crawl through
- Simple playhouses
- Balls and T-ball equipment

3 to 5 Years

Many of the previous, plus:

- Props that encourage role-playing
- Suitable surfaces for riding bikes, tricycles, and scooters
- Ladders and climbing structures
- Balance beams
- More-challenging slides
- Gliders and belt swings
- Kiddie pool for wading and splashing
- Chalk and a surface for drawing
- Sleds for cold climates
- Sport equipment

6 to 9 Years

Most of the previous, plus:

- Garden crafts kits and materials, including natural (pinecones, seashells) and artificial ones (terra-cotta pots, craft paint)
- Tire swings
- Forts
- Taller climbing structures and walls
- More-challenging slides
- Spaces to plant seeds and harvest produce
- Larger pool for swimming and water games
- More-advanced sport equipment; footballs, soccer balls, baseballs, and bats

10 to 13 Years

Most of the previous, plus:

- Elaborate forts and tree houses, especially those they help build
- Cable rides
- Challenging climbing structures and walls
- Ball courts and flat, open lawns for games
- A vegetable and flower garden of their own
- Putting green

14 Years and Older

Much of the previous, plus:

- Open lawns and equipment for group games like volleyball, football, or soccer
- Ramp for skateboarding and bike tricks

DESIGNING FOR PLAY

AS YOU PREPARE YOUR BACKYARD FOR SOME SERIOUS PLAY, think about balancing your kids' needs and your own. Separate play spaces physically or visually from areas where you and your spouse plan to relax or tend to a garden. And just as you have to childproof your house, you also have to keep child safety in mind in the backyard. Before you settle on a particular spot for your kids to play, consider the following elements:

- **SIZE.** Make sure the area, whether it is going to include a sandbox or a pool, is large enough for the number of children who will usually play there and the types of activities planned.

Stone dining patio

Sand area

Lawn

Vegetable garden

Rabbit hutch

Rubber play surface

Even a modest backyard can accommodate a range of activities when spaces are clearly defined.

- **SUN EXPOSURE.** How much sun does the area get during the day in the summer versus winter, and during a typical spring day? If it's too intense, you may want to build a canopy for shade or select another area.

- **CLEARANCE.** For safety, have at least 6 feet of space in all directions between the perimeter of any play structure and fencing or other structures in the yard. (See Safety Considerations, page 82, for more details.)

You can set kids' areas apart from adult spaces—yet keep them within your sight—in different ways. Designate distinct areas with physical borders, such as a wood rim around a sandbox, or with landing material, such as pea gravel or soft wood chips. You can also use stepping-stones or paths as dividers. Tree houses, playhouses, and other structures give children a private spot of their own. Whatever device you choose, make sure the borders you create don't prevent you from getting to kids quickly when they suffer the inevitable fall or scrape.

OPPOSITE: **In a well-planned space, multiple activities can unfold. The borders of an inground trampoline carve out one shady area. A safe distance away, a tree swing offers another timeless pleasure.**

Out of Sight: A Word About Storage

Before all of your great ideas for play, gardening, and other activities fill your backyard completely, consider setting aside a portion for storage. Many backyards have sheds or other structures for storing tools, garden supplies, and other items that don't fit in the garage or are too messy to go in the house. A separate structure can also protect toys and yard equipment from the elements.

If you have a lot of things to store, you can build a shed, buy a prefab one, or hire a pro. Ask at a home-improvement store for help in figuring out what materials (metal, vinyl, or wood) work best for your needs. Metal sheds, which come in a wide range of sizes and styles, are relatively low-cost but more prone to rust and dents. Sheds made of wood are sturdy and attractive, but also more expensive than metal and vulnerable to weather damage. Vinyl sheds resist damage best, but come in only a few sizes.

A shed need not interfere with the beauty of your backyard; for example, you can purchase one that looks like a red barn or that matches the style and color of your home. If you plan to build a playhouse, consider one that you can easily retrofit as a storage shed when your kids outgrow it.

WORKING WITH WOOD

NOW THAT WOOD INFUSED WITH AN ARSENIC-BASED PRESERVATIVE has been banned for most residential uses, there's no reason to be squeamish about using pressure-treated lumber on your kids' play structure. Several new kinds of pressure-treated lumber are now available, including ones preserved with organic insecticides and fungicides. Options also include plastic lumber and plastic-wood composites (see pages 12 to 13).

For play structures, the natural alternatives, such as cedar and redwood, are still the most appealing. Be aware, however, that the second-growth cedar and redwood on sale today are not as durable as old-growth lumber was. If you choose these species, select pieces with the darkest color for places where rot resistance matters most, such as parts in contact with soil. The whitish sections of cedar or redwood are no more rot resistant than ordinary pine.

In all types of pressure-treated lumber, the protection extends only to the shell of the wood. Builders must paint cut ends with a preservative, such as copper naphthenate. Otherwise, insects and the fungi that cause rot can simply tunnel into the wood through the exposed untreated fibers.

Below are some options for rot-resistant lumber. Ask your lumber dealer what's best for backyard use in your area.

• ACQ. Alkaline copper quaternary is a popular type of pressure-treated wood. The lumber contains copper and a chloride that together corrode galvanized coatings. Use stainless-steel fasteners where safety or appearance matters.

Green Lumber

If you're concerned about the environmental impact of using the wood you're considering for your play structure, visit the Forest Stewardship Council at www.fscus.org. This nonprofit organization works with an impressive group of major retailers (including Home Depot and Lowe's), as well as more than 600 builders and suppliers in the United States, to promote the

sustainable harvest of timber. Approved products bear an FSC label.

Southern pine　　Red cedar　　CA-B　　Redwood　　ACQ

- **CA-B.** This type of pressure-treated lumber is usually called "copper azole." The B stands for boric acid, which reduces the corrosive effect of the copper on fasteners. Hot-dipped galvanized fasteners and those with ceramic coatings are fine.
- **DOUGLAS FIR.** It's the most expensive treated-wood option, and may not be easy to find.
- **HEM-FIR.** Includes hemlock and five types of fir, but the strength of these boards varies.
- **RED CEDAR.** Similar to redwood but less splintery, red cedar contains tannins, which means that iron in the coating of hot-dipped galvanized fasteners can react with the tannins and leave dark stains. Aluminum fasteners work well but aren't widely available except as nails. Stainless-steel fasteners are best.
- **REDWOOD.** An old standby that today comes from second-growth stands. Also contains tannins, so choose fasteners as you would for red cedar.
- **SOUTHERN PINE.** A strong treated wood but susceptible to cracking.

Stainless steel

Galvanized

Aluminum

Fasteners

If you opt for pressure-treated wood, be sure to ask the supplier which type of fasteners to use. Many of the preservatives in pressure-treated lumber contain copper, which in wet conditions can cause a battery-like reaction that strips the zinc right off of galvanized fasteners, allowing them to rust. Electrogalvanized screws and nails, which appear shiny and smooth, do no better. Even the thicker, dull-gray coating on hot-dipped galvanized fasteners may not last long when in contact with some types of pressure-treated materials. Be prepared to spend a few extra bucks on stainless-steel fasteners, especially in locations where failure of the fastener would be a safety hazard.

Protecting Wood

Wood that occasionally gets wet but quickly dries usually doesn't rot. Its major enemy is more likely to be the sun's ultraviolet light, which breaks down lignin, the "glue" that holds wood fibers together. Over time, UV rays can leave wood looking dry and feeling rough and splintery. Stains and paints prevent this damage because their pigments block UV rays. Stains generally are easier to keep up because they don't peel. They are definitely the best choice for horizontal surfaces out in the weather, where paint can trap moisture within the wood, leading to decay.

SYNTHETIC MATERIALS

MORE PLAY STRUCTURES ARE BEING BUILT WITH NONWOOD MATERIALS. HERE'S HOW TO SELECT AND WORK WITH SYNTHETIC PRODUCTS

In addition to wood decking and railings, backyard structures can be constructed in whole or in part of synthetic materials. These materials, which range from composites of plastic and wood to boards made entirely of vinyl, are generally expensive, but the payoff is that they are virtually maintenance free. Or at least some of them are. While it is certainly true that synthetics are easier to care for than wood, be aware that not all synthetics perform the same, and no synthetic is perfect.

Currently, there are more than 80 manufacturers producing synthetic decking and railing materials. Note that synthetics can only be used for decking, railing, and decorative elements; they are not strong enough to be rated as structural members.

To choose the right synthetic product for your play structure, talk with neighbors, the staff at building-supply stores that sell several types of synthetics, and professional builders to learn how different products perform in your area. Some products have a fairly smooth surface; others have a deeply embossed wood-grain pattern. Still other products have variegated colors to further imitate the look of wood.

Composite hardwood

How to Choose

Composites are the most common type of synthetic. Composed of recycled plastic and ground-up waste wood, composites are an ecologically sound choice. At least three types of plastic are used in composite materials: standard polyethylene, which is fairly soft, polypropylene, and high-density polyethylene (HDPE).

Composites engineered with the last two kinds of plastic are harder and more stain- and scratch-resistant than composites containing polyethylene. The wood particles in many composites are not, as you might expect, entirely shielded from moisture, which means many composites are subject to mildew and fungus. To eliminate this problem, some products use a process that encapsulates the wood fibers.

All-vinyl decking has no wood particles, and is usually made with virgin rather than recycled plastic. These products are

Composite softwood

generally more expensive than composites, but they resist staining and fading better. The tradeoff is that they tend not to achieve a convincing wood-like appearance—most don't even try.

When choosing a synthetic, consider these factors:

- FADING. Some synthetics fade faster than others. Of those that do, many can be painted to restore their original color.
- FASTENERS. Buy your fasteners when you buy your synthetic lumber. Railing systems are usually sold with their own special clips; some brands of decking require invisible fastening systems.
- MILDEW. Just because a product is synthetic doesn't mean it won't mildew, especially in humid climates or shady locations.
- MUSHROOMS. Driving a nail or screw through a synthetic board usually produces a small raised bump, or mushroom, around the screw head (top right). In many cases, these mushrooms can be virtually eliminated by tapping them lightly with a hammer (right).

- SCRATCHING. Synthetics scratch fairly easily, although some are engineered for scratch resistance. You can erase scratches with a heat gun, but try this technique on a sample first.
- STAINING. Grease from food and rust from toys left out in the rain may produce stains that are difficult to remove.
- SWELLING. All synthetics swell at least slightly; some swell a lot. Be sure to leave gaps between boards as specified by the manufacturer.

Pros and Cons of Plastics

Plastic and composite lumber are suitable for decking on play structures, but synthetic materials are not as strong as most natural lumber. If you are running decking on a play platform at an angle, for example, this may mean that you will need to space the joists closer together than with wood decking. Don't forget to factor this in when comparing the cost of synthetic materials to wood. Plastic and composite lumber also don't have the stiffness needed for posts, joists, and deck rails. Yes, the materials are free of splinters and generally require little or no maintenance, but they can be heavy, which may require beefing up the support structure. And some types, especially those with dark colors, absorb so much heat that they can be unpleasant to play on when the sun's out. Buy a small piece and leave it out in the sun to test this for yourself before you build.

BUILDING WITH KIDS

WITH SOME GUIDANCE AND A LOT OF PATIENCE FROM YOU, YOUR KIDS CAN BE A REAL HELP IN ANY PROJECT. WATCH THEIR CHESTS SWELL WITH PRIDE WHEN THEY PROCLAIM, "I BUILT THIS!"

A project may take a bit longer when you involve your child in the building process, but it will be a rewarding experience for both of you.

It sounds great to involve kids in building their own play spaces, but the reality is that it's often a frustrating experience for children and adults alike. Keep in mind that the first stages often go slower than everyone expects, which can get things off on a sour note. Pace projects so that when kids are there to help, there's something useful for them to do. For example, have the kids help clear and stake out the site, then they can go off to do something else while the adults fine-tune the foundation. When the actual building commences, get the kids involved again.

Whether you build a project from scratch or buy a do-it-yourself kit from a lumberyard or home center, this is an excellent opportunity for kids to help out by following directions and assembling pieces. If you hire a professional builder, however, kids need to stay out of the way during the building process. They can still get involved by choosing the swing set's components or by planting a garden next to the playhouse.

Sawing and Hammering

Children are often eager to cut wood and pound nails, two jobs that seem like the essence of building. To make headway with a handsaw requires both a sharp blade and a way to hold the wood steady. Young children will need to clamp the wood to a work surface, which should be a little lower than waist height. (If the workbench is higher, have a stepstool handy.) Instruct them to saw with both hands on the handle, even though a professional would never do it this way. They'll make faster progress, won't tire as easily, and can't cut themselves.

Older kids can saw the standard way, gripping the tool with one hand. If clamps aren't handy, show them how to use their body to hold the wood down, just as carpenters often do. Place the wood on a slightly elevated surface, such as a milk crate or a deck step, and have the child hold the piece in place with the knee or foot opposite the sawing arm.

For children who want to pound nails, here are a few tips that may lead to more success. First, have them—not you—hold the nail, and tell them to keep their eyes on it as they hammer. (It's eye-hand coordination that keeps people from smashing their own fingers.) Kids should give the nail a few taps to set it, then move their hand away so they can drive the nail home with successively harder blows.

Coach children to position themselves so they can swing the hammer in an arc to one side of their body. When kids hammer in front of their belly, the nail usually bends. It's okay if kids instinctively grip midway on the handle, especially if they're young or the hammer is heavy. They'll gain in control what they sacrifice in force, which will come later.

The easiest kind of nailing is straight down. Good tasks for kids include nailing floorboards and assembling parts that can be laid out on a flat surface. If kids don't have the strength to drive nails, try helping them to use a drill and screws instead.

Let him hold the nail—it's hand-eye coordination that keeps him from hitting his fingers with the hammer.

Tips on Drilling

Older kids enjoy using a power drill to prepare joints so that they won't have protruding bolts or nuts, which can cause nasty cuts. To allow use of bolts whose length matches the thickness of the wood being fastened, oversize holes, called counterbores, need to be drilled on the back of the wood. Young children can't keep a drill straight and steady enough for the wide bit that's needed for the counterbore, but middle school–age kids usually can.

Bolted connections call for carriage bolts, which have rounded heads. So that sharp bolt ends don't protrude on the back, drill a recess for the nut before you drill the bolt hole. Use a spade bit that makes a hole wide enough for a socket wrench and add masking tape as a depth stop, set to the thickness of the nut and washer. The center point guides a twist bit

($\frac{1}{16}$ inch wider than the bolt) the rest of the way through. A scrap block underneath keeps the exit hole from tearing.

In addition, have kids predrill all screw holes; it's hard for them to put enough pressure on a drill to get self-drilling screws to seat properly.

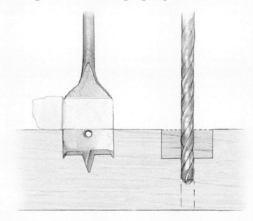

JOBS AND TOOLS

THE TOOLS YOUR KIDS USE AND THE WORK THEY DO largely depend on their age as well as their strength and maturity. Here's a guide to keeping the job site safe and fun.

3 to 5 years

- Help design
- Hand nails or tools
- Fetch things
- Shovel sand or pea gravel
- Paint
- Help decorate
- Help clean up

PAD AND PAINTBRUSH Inexpensive brushes work best for small projects because they can be washed easily. For big expanses, avoid spatters by using paint pads instead of rollers.

BUCKET Use buckets to carry tools, sand, and dirt. Avoid the 5-gallon size, whose dimensions present a drowning hazard to toddlers.

TOOL BELT Though not essential, it's useful for keeping nails and screws close at hand, and kids like the look. A junior-size one makes toting tools more manageable.

Safety

For general job-site safety, make sure there are plenty of adult helpers in proportion to the number of kids involved. One adult can supervise two children, but if the ratio is higher and the kids are young, they often wind up waiting for advice on how to proceed. While they wait, accidents can happen.

Start by putting all the tools in one place, and showing kids which ones they can touch or use and which ones they can't. Then explain, step by step, what you are doing, so kids know what to expect. Good communication can help keep young minds from wandering.

A safety note for all ages: Never use electric power tools in the rain or when the ground is wet.

GLOVES If you can't find kid-size work gloves, look for stretchy gardeners' gloves.

GOGGLES Eye protection is a must whenever power tools are used.

EAR PROTECTORS Many kids are especially sensitive to the noise of power tools. In addition to ear plugs, adult-size earmuffs usually adjust to fit.

6 to 7 years

All of the previous, plus:

- Hold tape measure
- Drill (with adult help)
- Tighten screws in pre-drilled holes
- Tighten bolts

- Sort parts
- Note and check measurements
- Help check for square angles
- Remove nails on salvaged lumber

TAPE MEASURE Contractors' tapes with 1-inch blades are too heavy and bulky to fit in a kid-size tool belt. Instead look for a half-inch blade with a tape no more than 12 feet long.

SCREWDRIVER Choose a 4-in-1 screwdriver that offers small and large bits in two styles, Phillips and straight.

8 to 11 years

All of the previous, plus:

- Nail, especially downward
- Mix concrete, but only one sack at a time
- Cut boards to length where angle isn't critical

CLAMPS For kids, it's just as it is with adults: You can never have too many.

SMALL HAMMER Find one under 12 ounces from a manufacturer that also makes hammers for pros—the domed faces to help nails go in straight.

CORDLESS DRILL A 12-volt version can be a good first power tool for older children to use.

RASP AND SANDING BLOCK Direct the rasp down and slightly forward to keep long splinters from forming. Smooth wood with a foam-type sanding block, which is easier for children to use than sandpaper.

WRENCHES Adjustable wrenches are handy, but a socket set with a ratchet socket is best when there are many bolts to tighten.

12 years and older

Depending on the kid, pretty much anything, including:

- More-complex saw cuts
- Power saw with jigsaw if wood is clamped and an adult is watching
- More independent drilling

JIGSAW Because there's no kickback and the blade is always within clear view, this is a power saw suitable for older kids with supervision. Makes curved or straight cuts.

HANDSAW Efficient sawing means using most of the blade on each cut, so the blade must not be too long for kids. A toolbox saw has a blade about 15 inches long. A pistol-grip saw sports a 12-inch blade.

DESIGNING FOR KIDS

BEING A KID IN AN ADULT WORLD means standing on a stepstool to turn on the faucet or climbing up onto a chair to reach something on a counter. But what if everything were just her size, from the door to the windows to even the roof? To make your yard truly magical for children, consider it from their perspective. For a kid's-eye view, squat at their level and take a look around. Then plan your projects with their ages and developmental stages in mind.

A pint-size playhouse—as modest as a 3-by-3-foot hut—will make even the smallest child feel big, and at the same time give him a private place to create imaginary worlds. Or a miniature picnic table can be the setting for tea parties and crafts. For older children, a roomier clubhouse, an elevated fort, or an adjustable basketball stand will stimulate changing abilities and interests.

Size also matters when it comes to safety. Any structure that you buy or build should meet basic child safety standards, which may differ by age. For example, to avoid mishaps, the Consumer Product Safety Commission suggests that the fall height from any platform be no greater than 30 inches for school-age children and even less for preschoolers— maxing out at 20 inches. See Safety Considerations, page 82, for more guidelines.

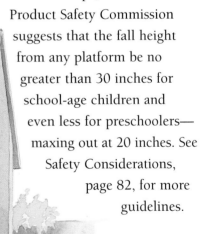

A playhouse that is scaled to a child is the perfect setting for imaginative adventures.

Landscaping for Play

Before you settle on any particular spot for a project or play area, step back and consider the whole yard, from its shape to its size. Make a drawing or site map of your lot, marking the dimensions and including any required distances between property lines, buildings, and structures. (Check regulations with your building department.) Once you've got a basic sketch, note details such as areas with strong sun or wind, the location of pipes and utility lines, and any trees and plants. This will help you pick the best site not only for a sandbox or ball court but for all of the different features in your yard, including a garden, a floating deck, or a koi pond.

As you take a close look at your map, consider the views and sight lines from all sides of the lot. You may want to do some or all of the following:

• MAKE SURE YOU CAN SUPERVISE the kids' play area from a deck or an inside room.

• REMOVE OBSTRUCTIONS such as a pole or an overgrown tree that could block your view.

• CONSIDER FOOT TRAFFIC through play, garden, and sitting areas.

• SCREEN UNDESIRABLE VIEWS to the street or a neighbor's home.

• BUILD A FENCE or plant hedges as a safety, privacy, and sound barrier.

Plan exactly how the play area will interact with other elements. Play sets, for example, should be a safe distance (at least 6 feet in all directions) from walls or rocks. You may also want to keep younger children separate from older kids' antics. Now is also the time to let your mind explore where you might design hideaways, meandering paths, and other extras that will make your backyard an everyday retreat for your whole family.

What Kid Size Means at Different Ages

AGE GROUP	DOORWAY HEIGHT	GUARDRAIL HEIGHT	RUNG SPACING*	CHIN BAR HEIGHT**	MINIMUM SEAT WIDTH
2–3½ years	32–43 inches	22–24 inches	9–18 inches	38–49 inches	6–9 inches
5½–6½ years	38–51 inches	22–29 inches	14–27 inches	46–62 inches	7–11 inches
11½–12½ years	52–69 inches	30–39 inches	18–31 inches	62–84 inches	9–16 inches

*on horizontal ladders, monkey bars
**where feet bottom out

SMALL YARDS

PLANNING FOR EXCITING PLAY OPPORTUNITIES is more challenging in a small yard, but it's not impossible. For example, you can place a sandbox under a raised clubhouse or erect a movable tent instead of a cottage. Kids seek out quiet retreats and places to hide, so even trees, shrubs, or tall flowers can provide "structures" they can play behind, in between, or beneath.

The yard's features can help steer activities, such as chalk-drawing on a concrete canvas of patio pavers. In a limited area, you may have less need for building hard-and-fast borders between adult and child areas and can instead allow bushy plants to serve that purpose. But if your kids—and you—want separate spaces, a modest tree house might do the trick. Additional small-yard play ideas include a portable putting green or a balance beam.

A multilevel, multifunction play set makes up for a lack of space. Younger kids can play in a shaded sandbox, while older kids can use a climbing ramp to reach the platform above.

Wood borders and soft landing materials set a child's play area apart. With the help of a slightly higher divider, a parent's garden grows not far away.

It's okay to draw on this wall, thanks to chalkboard paint, which turned a blank expanse into a creative canvas.

Another strategy for allowing a small space to accommodate big ideas is to designate a sizable portion for play. A large play structure, such as a swing set with a climbing wall or a log fort with a bridge, may take up some room, but it can serve multiple purposes. Or an open lawn can serve as the setting for different sports at different times. Be sure to take measurements and plan enough space so you and the kids can enjoy activities safely.

Pavers and a sandbox create areas for cycling and sand play without disturbing shrubs and flowers. A swing is just a stone's throw away.

ADDING EXTRAS

SOMETIMES IT'S THE LITTLE THINGS IN A BACKYARD that make the biggest difference to kids. For example, a water fountain is easy to create and adds beauty and a soundtrack to your garden. Or consider an outdoor shower for washing off before or after a swim, or just to keep cool on a hot day. Another possibility is to create a special habitat where kids can tend to a furry friend.

Rachel can rinse her hands clean and get a kick out of the details on this ornamental fountain.

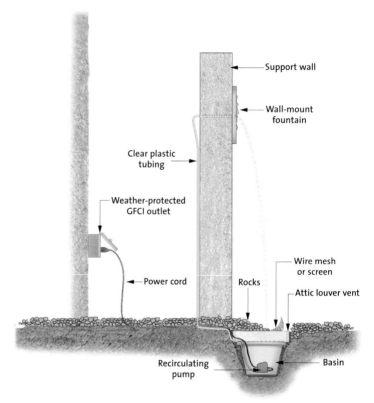

Support wall

Wall-mount fountain

Clear plastic tubing

Weather-protected GFCI outlet

Power cord

Rocks

Wire mesh or screen

Attic louver vent

Recirculating pump

Basin

You can buy a fountain and a recirculating pump as part of a set, or purchase parts individually. Check the pump's label to make sure it's capable of lifting water as high as you want, and be sure to buy tubing that's the diameter specified by the pump's manufacturer. The pump, which sits in the basin, pushes water up to the fountain through the tubing, which is hidden behind the wall that supports the fountain.

Splish splash, they're taking an outdoor bath! A shower constructed from existing plumbing lines near the house can help cut down on the need for pool chemicals if kids rinse off before taking a dip. At right, water appears to flow from a stone.

A cozy hutch tucked beneath a deck provides easy access for kids to hold, stroke, and feed bunnies or other small animals.

A CHILD'S GARDEN

PICTURE YOUR IDEAL FAMILY GARDEN AND WHAT MIGHT BE IN IT. Hardy grasses and shrubs can provide a beautiful, natural landscape for play. With colorful perennial and annual flowers, you can have both a calming view and the pleasure of cutting flowers for indoor display. Add a plot of vegetables and some fruit trees to the mix, and you've got fresh edibles for all to pick and enjoy.

A great garden just takes a little bit of planning. To get started, sit down as a family to list and prioritize goals. Do you plan on growing produce or just flowers? Do your kids want their own vegetable patch or a butterfly garden? Will a pet need its own territory? Answering these questions will help you organize the garden into sections by function.

A canopy of brightly colored *Thunbergia alata* (black-eyed Susan vine) creates an entryway for this budding naturalist tending her flock.

PLANTS TO ENJOY

Bush beans
Grows fast, edible

Cosmos
Attracts hummingbirds

Fuchsias
Choose hanging varieties

Herbs
Edible, easy to grow

Hollyhocks
Grows tall for visual impact

Lamb's ear
Velvety to the touch, easy to grow

Nasturtiums
Edible, easy to grow

Ornamental corn
Fun to harvest

Pansies
Edible flowers

Pumpkins, gourds
Good for crafting

Raspberries, blackberries
Edible, perennial

Snapdragons
Attracts hummingbirds

Strawberries
Edible, easy to grow in pots

Summer squash
Grows fast, edible

Sunflowers
Grows fast, variety of sizes

Tomatoes
Choose cherry or dwarf sizes

Now consider how much time you want to spend on maintenance. Trees and shrubs require less care than flowers. But after the initial work of preparing a plot and planting, tending to flowers or vegetables may take less time than you might think—just a few hours a week.

Before you choose the plants, first research online, at the library, or at a nursery which ones are best suited to your climate and the conditions in your yard. Refer to books such as the *Sunset Western Garden Book*, a resource of more than 8,000 plants for gardeners nationwide. If you're a novice gardener, also gather tips on irrigation, soil, planting, and fertilizing. While you're at it, take the time to introduce kids to the many colors, textures, and life cycles of the plants that will inhabit their yard.

Kid-Friendly Planting

As you plan and plant your garden, keep in mind that gardening is more art than science. Choose plants that appeal to you and your family, but be open to unusual forms, textures, and colors. If you already have plants, add ones with varying shapes or leaf sizes. Think beyond common flowers and look for plants that will be a delight for kids to discover, eat, or use for crafts. Also use the opportunity to instill appreciation for the environment by teaching kids about how plants help provide clean air, how birds and insects play a role in plant life, and water use and conservation.

PLANTS TO AVOID

Bougain-villea
Spikey thorns on vines

Brugmansia
All parts are poisonous

Cactus
Thorns; choose thornless prickly pear

Chrysanthe-mums
Leaves and stalks can cause rash

Daffodils
Poisonous bulbs

Delphiniums
All parts are poisonous

Foxglove
Poisonous flowers, leaves, and seeds

Holly
Poisonous berries, sharp leaves

Hydrangeas
Poisonous flowers and buds

Mistletoe
Poisonous berries

Mountain laurel
Poisonous leaves and nectar

Oleander
All parts are poisonous

Rhubarb
Poisonous leaves

Roses
Thorns of various sizes

Sweet peas
Poisonous seeds

Wisteria
All parts are poisonous, especially seeds

GARDENS FOR KIDS

GO BEYOND THE CONVENTIONAL and experiment with fanciful amenities to entice children into the garden. To uncover unique finds, visit flea markets, architectural salvage yards, toy stores, and even your own attic. Think about features that will attract birds and butterflies, and encourage your kids to do the planting and watering. Along the way, they may even learn a thing or two about nature and their backyard environment.

LEFT: **Turn a border area into a locale for learning the alphabet and the names of plants, with colorful letters that appear to grow out of the ground.** BELOW: **Instead of just one birdhouse, mount a collection to create a focal point behind flowers. These wooden ones blend nicely with the siding and trellises.**

A variety of fast-growing plants will keep kids engaged during the growing season. Add some whimsical elements, like these brightly colored rain boots in lieu of pots for planting, and kids won't be able to resist.

ABOVE: What are these dishes doing in a bed of sweet alyssum? Soaking in the sink, of course! What better way to put old dishes to use? RIGHT: Teach children to care for plants—and not trample on them—with decorative markers such as this one, which features an artichoke below the letter A.

THE FAMILY SWIMMING HOLE

MORE THAN MOST BACKYARD AMENITIES, A POOL SERVES MANY FAMILY FUNCTIONS. Children can learn to swim in it or just cool off on a hot day. Adults can get a rigorous workout or take a peaceful dip. A pool can also enhance the beauty of your landscape and provide a serene backdrop for garden parties.

With pools and ponds, always put safety first. Supervise children while they're swimming and maintain a clear view of the entire pool from a deck or patio. To prevent kids from gaining access when adults are not around, install a guardrail or fence that is at least 48 inches from the ground with no handholds or footholds that would allow a child to climb over. Pool gates should open out from the poolside and be self-latching or -closing. Also install an alarm or self-closing device on any doors that lead to the pool area. Remove or block access to deck ladders for aboveground pools when they are not in use.

Install a safety cover. Varieties include netting with holes too small for an infant to fall through, a strong polypropylene mesh anchored to the sides of the pool, and a solid vinyl surface that you can roll out.

Consider water disturbance or wristband alarms that sound when a child is in the pool. And always keep lifesaving gear, such as life preservers, a shepherd's pole, and rope, nearby.

A backyard pool is a sure-fire draw for your children and their friends, which means your kids' social scene happens where you can keep an eye on them.

A safety fence around the pool need not detract from backyard beauty. With the right materials, it can blend in with your décor.

Pool covers are perhaps the most important safety feature. There are several types to suit your pool and personal taste. Automatic-cover systems, like the one on this infinity-edge pool and adjacent spa (above), provide safety with the flip of a switch. Less expensive options include netting or mesh covers (left) that can be stretched over a spa or pool of any shape and size.

Pond Protection

It's easy to forget that a pond is as much a potential hazard for young children as a large pool. Even a small, shallow pond poses a risk to infants and toddlers, who can lose their balance and fall in. To protect top-heavy little ones, install a pond cover. The one featured here creates an above-water grid surface. Other types can be submerged under water and look almost invisible. These safety covers can be designed to fit any pond shape and are often made strong enough for even an adult to stand on. Fish and other wildlife won't be affected—and herons won't be able to get to your koi.

structures

THE BEST STRUCTURES ARE PLACES WHERE KIDS CAN
INVENT ROLES AND ACT OUT ADVENTURES. TO CREATE
THE ULTIMATE PLAY STRUCTURE, INVOLVE CHILDREN
FROM PLANNING TO BUILDING TO DECORATING. USE
THIS CHAPTER TO EXPLORE DIFFERENT TYPES AND
MATERIALS, AND TO DECIDE WHETHER TO BUY A KIT
OR HIRE A PRO. YOU'LL ALSO FIND A RANGE OF
PROJECTS YOU CAN BUILD YOURSELF.

PLAYHOUSE PRIMER

ALTHOUGH NUMEROUS PLAYHOUSE KITS ARE AVAILABLE, anyone with a few spare weekends, a reasonable supply of common tools, and some basic carpentry skills should be able to build one from scratch. Here are the basic construction methods:

Standard Stud Construction

Build a skeleton from 2 × 4s, 2 × 3s, or, for a small playhouse, even 1 × 2s. Then cover the framing with roofing and siding. This is probably the best method to use on playhouses that will later be converted to permanent structures in the garden or guest houses.

1. Build the floor first, then frame the walls on it.
2. Assemble walls horizontally so you can drive nails through the base and top plates into studs. Install windows while walls are still flat.
3. Make side walls as long as the floor. End walls should be the width of the floor minus the thickness of the two side walls.
4. Prop up one side wall, nail it to the floor, and brace it diagonally so it stays upright. Then prop up an end wall and fasten it to the floor and to the side wall. Add the other two walls.
5. Build the roof in place. Start by tacking uprights to temporarily support a ridge beam. Install the ridge beam, then each pair of rafters.

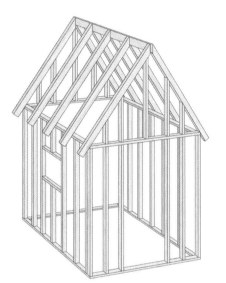

STANDARD STUD CONSTRUCTION

Plywood Shell

This method works well when a playhouse or fort is built at one location and then assembled elsewhere. It's also a good choice for a structure that will later be taken apart and moved.

1. For floors, use ¾-inch plywood or a double layer of ⅜ inch. Walls and roof can be ⅜ inch or ½ inch.
2. Lay out walls so they make efficient use of plywood, which generally comes in sheets 4 by 8 feet. Trim the floor to fit with the wall dimensions; you'll make fewer cuts.
3. Screws and nails don't hold well when they are driven into the end grain of plywood. Beef up such connections by adding a piece of solid wood (at least 1 × 2s) to the rear plywood piece so the screw has something firm to grab.
4. For easy, perfectly hung doors and window shutters, cut the plywood only along the hinge line of these openings. Stop and add hinges. Then cut out the rest of the opening.

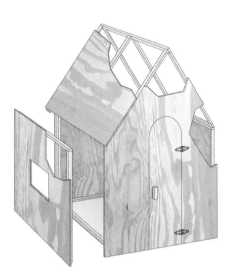

PLYWOOD SHELL

Pole Building

Borrowing from a popular method for building barns, set posts into the ground and use them for both the foundation and the corner posts of the playhouse or fort. This is the easiest, fastest construction method. It's especially suitable for structures that parents frame but kids finish (see pages 40 to 41).

1. Set pressure-treated posts into the ground at least 2 feet deep or below the frost line. Secure with either concrete or sharp-edged gravel packed tight.
2. Bolt rim joists onto the posts to support the floor and the roof.
3. Add vertical wall framing where necessary, including on both sides of doors and windows, and frame the roof.
4. Add roofing, siding, and trim.

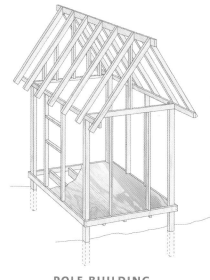

POLE BUILDING

Foundations

A playhouse or fort doesn't need a full-scale foundation, but there must still be a way to keep the floor dry and the siding off the ground. Setting a playhouse on an existing paved patio may seem like a simple solution, but if the paving extends beyond the walls, water will almost surely get in.

Set the floor joists on pier blocks (left) or standard concrete blocks. Fastening temporary buildings to the blocks isn't crucial because the weight of the structures holds them in place.

To Build or Buy?

Building a playhouse can be lots of fun or a nightmare that seems to go on and on. When time or skill is short, a variety of kits and ready-made solutions are worth considering.

• **STORAGE SHEDS.** Prefab storage sheds sold at home centers can easily be retrofitted as playhouses. Kits include all lumber and fasteners but not foundations.

• **PARTIALLY ASSEMBLED PLAYHOUSE KIT.** The kit from Practical Folly Playhouses (top right) features a Dutch door and an interior ladder to the belfry lookout. It's shipped with floor, wall, and roof sections ready to be screwed into place. Costs for kits like this vary widely. Check to see if the prices you're quoted include shipping, fasteners, and a foundation.

• **CUSTOM-BUILT PLAYHOUSE.** Scaled for kids but with all the bells and whistles of a standard house, this custom-built playhouse from La Petite Maison (bottom right) features a finished interior and wrap-around porch. High-end playhouses like this one can cost about the same as a mid-sized car.

ABOVE AND TOP: **Shaded by leafy trees, this charming little cabin is shingled on the outside and decked out with comfy chairs, a soft rug, and homey elements inside, making it the perfect preteen escape.**

A GALLERY OF GREAT PLACES

ABOVE: **Nature supplied the foundation for this lofty playhouse. The wooden steps are steep, so a railing was installed for safety.**

WHAT MAKES A GREAT TREE HOUSE OR PLAY STRUCTURE? Surely, not size, complexity, or expense, as a humble cabin can provide endless opportunities for fun. It's the love and time that went into building it, or the peaceful location, or the way it brings family members and friends together.

By incorporating natural materials and colors, and integrating with landscape, structures like tree houses, forts, and playhouses can coexist with other backyard elements. Or build a structure that both kids and adults can enjoy, like a deck with a tree growing through it (opposite, top).

If you don't want a full tree house, consider these two unusual options. Instead of a playhouse set in tree branches, create an entire deck and roof around a large tree (far left). A wooden bench encircles the trunk. Or build a spiral staircase leading up to a tree house (left) that is essentially an elevated deck.

BELOW: This play set looks like anything but. Built atop rock walls and columns, it gives a typical children's structure a more sophisticated appearance. Kids can climb, swing, and slide in a lovely rustic landscape, while adults can hang out in Adirondack chairs below.

BUILDING IN TREES

WITH A TREE HOUSE, THE FOUNDA-
TION IS THE TRICKIEST DETAIL. ONCE
IT'S DONE, THE REST OF THE CON-
STRUCTION IS FAIRLY STANDARD

Tree houses can be supported by one, two, three, or more trees, or even by trees plus posts set into the ground. Nails or screws won't hurt a tree, as long as they are not spaced closely together. But trees can be injured if a chain or rope girdles the trunk or if a tree house rubs against the bark. Because trees bend in the wind and grow wider over the years, foundations must be built to flex as needed. In a pushing match, trees always beat tree houses.

When a single tree supports a tree house, the floor or deck usually circles the trunk (top left). Attach each of the two main beams to the trunk with a single bolt, or use a custom-made fitting as shown on page 73. Add rim joists, attaching them to each other but not to the two main supports so that the floor can slide as the tree grows wider. Then install diagonal bracing to keep the floor from tipping. Only once those are in place is it safe to climb onto the framing and finish the floor. These details are more fully explored starting on page 70.

Four trees or a combination of trees and posts can be used like corner posts to support a tree house (bottom left). Small structures close to the ground can rest on two beams bolted to the trees. Larger or higher tree houses should rest on supports that allow the base to move as the trees grow and sway in the wind. To create a flexible foundation, bolt only one end of each support beam to a tree. Support the other end with a connection that allows movement. One solution, shown in more detail on page 78, allows the support beam to rest on a large lag bolt driven only partway into the trunk. A malleable iron washer acts as a stop.

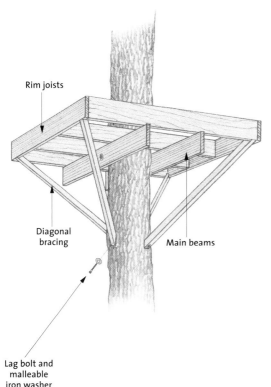

Rim joists

Diagonal
bracing

Main beams

Lag bolt and
malleable
iron washer

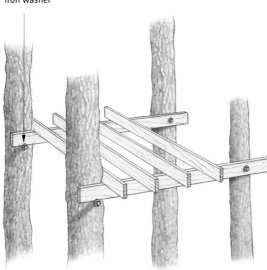

Getting Up and Down

Climbing up and down a ladder is half the fun of a tree house or raised fort. When designing a ladder, there are two key safety factors. First, make openings smaller than $3\frac{1}{2}$ inches or larger than 9 inches. Even if your kids are past the age when you need to worry about them squeezing through a $3\frac{1}{2}$-inch opening, there's no point building something that may endanger another child some day. If a staircase needs steps between those measurements, close off the opening between the treads.

Also, space rungs or treads uniformly. People can easily adjust to varied step heights when they scramble over rocks. But when climbing a staircase or ladder, even young children subconsciously gauge the distance between the first couple of steps and are likely to stumble if the following steps aren't exactly the same.

Long, sturdy pieces of plywood and boards can be turned into ramps. Screw cleats near the ends so the boards have a lip that can be slipped over boxes, ladder rungs, or other parts of a play structure. The lip adds stability and helps to keep pieces from slipping.

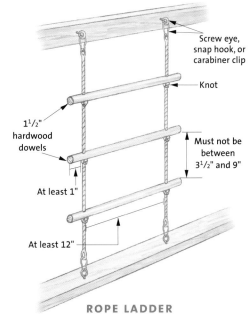

Screw eye, snap hook, or carabiner clip

Knot

$1\frac{1}{2}$" hardwood dowels

At least 1"

Must not be between $3\frac{1}{2}$" and 9"

At least 12"

ROPE LADDER
Attach top and bottom for easier climbing.

Finish nails keep rungs from spinning

RUNG LADDER

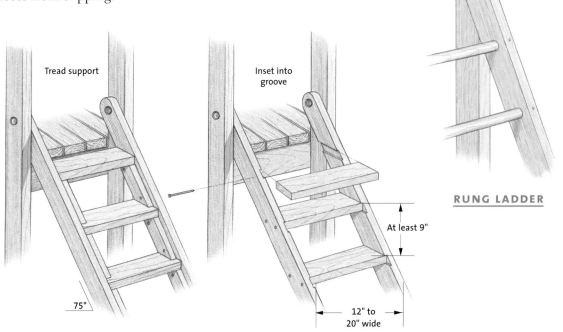

Tread support

Inset into groove

75°

At least 9"

12" to 20" wide

LADDERS
The best angle is 75 degrees from the ground.
Support treads with wood, not just nails or screws.

ROOFING AND SIDING

ONCE YOU'VE GOT YOUR FOUNDA-TION SQUARED AWAY, the next steps are building the walls and raising the roof. Read on for tips and techniques for installing metal roofing as well as for creating board-and-batten and plywood-and-batten siding.

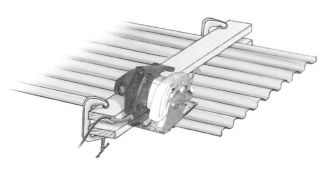

Metal Roofing

Inexpensive and quick to install, metal roofing looks great and lets kids enjoy the *plink-plink* of falling rain. Screws with neoprene washers seal out the moisture. Choose galvanized roofing if you want a rustic look or painted styles for a more finished look. Use full-length pieces if possible. If not, cut panels using a circular saw fitted with either a special metal-cutting blade or a noncarbide blade set backward. Since metal roofing flexes, provide support so the blade doesn't bend. Wear safety goggles for the glowing metal shards, ear protectors for the screech, and gloves for the sharp edges. Install so the cut edges are hidden under the roof cap.

Board-and-Batten Siding

These patterned walls give a playhouse or fort a country-cabin feel. If the walls are less than 6 feet tall, you may be able to save money by using good-quality fence boards rather than standard lumber. But be aware that fence boards may contain too much moisture to be painted right away and will later shrink considerably. Also, avoid boards with loose knots.

With any type of wood, board-and-batten siding must be installed so the boards won't split when they expand and contract as humidity fluctuates. Provide plenty of overlap—at least $3/4$ inch for 4-inch boards and more for wider ones. Nail wide boards only along one edge, and leave at least a nail's width between fence boards or up to $1/2$ inch with dry lumber, so that the wood can move without splitting. The battens will hold the other edge in place. Batten nails fit into the spaces between the wide boards. This style of wall is typically built with wide boards and thin battens, but you can also use boards of equal width; just leave more space between them.

Because vertical boards absorb water along their bottom edge, increasing the risk of rot, coat the ends of boards liberally with a water-repellent preservative. Pick a preservative that is paintable if you plan to add a finish to the wall.

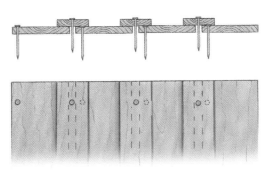

Plywood with Battens

Adding thin vertical trim boards to simple plywood walls dresses them up considerably and mimics the look of true board-and-batten siding. If you want to stain or paint the battens a different color than the underlying wall, apply the finishes before installation. Space the battens evenly and so that one is positioned over every joint where sheets of plywood meet. To avoid splitting thin battens and to hold both sheets in place, stagger the placement of the nails.

Recycled Materials

Incorporating second-hand and discarded materials saves natural resources, gives the structures an instant patina, and helps them look like individual creations rather than mass-produced toys. Salvage dealers offer everything from lumber to stair parts to decorative hardware—check your phone directory or the Web for local sources. Smaller detail pieces can usually be shipped cheaply.

If you are lucky enough to live near a good architectural salvage warehouse, take the time to wander a bit and think about how different parts may be employed unconventionally. Maybe those beautiful balusters could be cut in half and turned into window trim. Or perhaps an old bed headboard could see a second life as a railing.

Creating a Store Door

A half door topped with a shelf creates a surface for a store countertop one day, a mail center or puppet stage the next. Select a solid-wood door that has a wide piece of wood going horizontally across the middle. Saw through this wood to cut the door in half, taking care to miss the doorknob hole. Screw wooden or metal brackets into the door to support the shelf. Locate them so that the top of the shelf will be flush with the top of the door section. Screw a 6-inch shelf board down into the brackets, and add a few screws that go horizontally through the door and into the shelf.

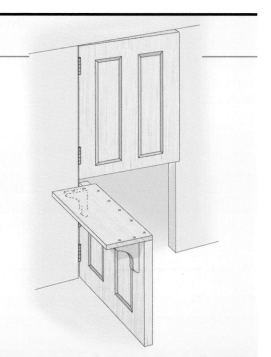

HOMEMADE PLAYHOUSE

FOUR STURDY POSTS IN THE GROUND AND AN ASSORTMENT OF COMMON MATERIALS ARE ALL SOME KIDS NEED TO BUILD THEIR OWN FORTS AND PLAYHOUSES

Jeff Powers and Debby Haase outfitted an old shed on their property as a playhouse, but their children rarely used it. Then Jeff framed a smaller structure and left it for Ken, 8, and Charlie, 11, to finish. Day after day, it occupied their attention as they hunted for leftover siding for the walls, fashioned a door out of scrap plywood, and rigged up a slide. When rain threatened, they even engineered a ditch to channel water away from the structure. "With the other playhouse, there wasn't anything left for them to do," Debby says. "With this one, they did it all."

Building materials can range from wood that's at least long enough to span the posts to salvaged window frames to old balusters as railings. The posts should be sturdy enough to withstand having a variety of things nailed to them, pulled out, and nailed back many times as whims change.

Older children may want to build on an elevated platform so they have a floor. For safe floor supports, help them bolt on thick planks, at least 2 by 6 inches. Recess the bolts (see page 15) or cover exposed ends with cap screws. Also ensure that there's a safe way up and down, if that's an issue.

Materials List

- Four pressure-treated 4 × 4 posts, each 6' to 8' long
- Four to six bags of ready-mix or fast-setting concrete, or sharp-edged gravel
- Building materials such as boards, nails, plywood, roofing paper, door hinges, and fabric

Building the Basic Structure

Dig oversized post holes 2 feet deep or below the frost line. With a level, adjust posts so they are perfectly vertical. Temporarily brace them in place.

Add concrete or gravel, tamping after each shovelful or two with a sturdy piece of wood or metal to remove air pockets. If you don't have enough material to fill the holes, use tamped earth or gravel near the top.

Concrete makes poles more rigid, but gravel is easier to remove when the playhouse is no longer an item of interest.

Getting It Square

Although kid-built forts don't have to be square, budding carpenters will probably appreciate posts set at right angles to one another. To do this, begin at the first post and measure out 3 feet in one direction and 4 feet at an approximate right angle. Adjust the end points until the distance between them equals 5 feet. Any point on the 3- or 4-foot lines will then be a suitable place for posts. About 4 feet apart works well (especially if you or the children will be cutting apart 8-foot boards to use for the fort itself). Locate the final post in a similar manner.

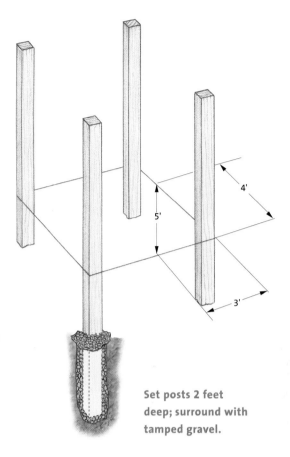

Set posts 2 feet deep; surround with tamped gravel.

More Fun Ideas

There's nothing like options to fuel a kid's imagination. Once you've built the basic structure, kids can go the playhouse route or construct one of these two alternatives.

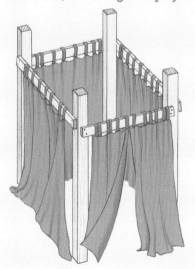

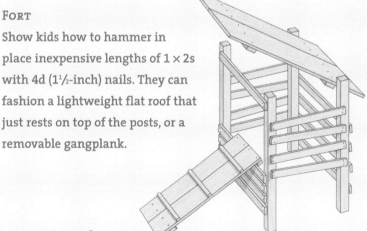

FORT

Show kids how to hammer in place inexpensive lengths of 1 × 2s with 4d (1½-inch) nails. They can fashion a lightweight flat roof that just rests on top of the posts, or a removable gangplank.

THEATER

Tie on sheets or curtains and let the kids put on a show.

A Cabin for Kids

AMISH CRAFTSMANSHIP LENDS AN AUTHENTIC FEEL TO THIS KID-SIZE CABIN. A LOFT INSIDE AND A BACK-DOOR INVITE THE WHOLE FAMILY INTO THIS HOME AWAY FROM HOME

The owners of this Los Gatos, California, cabin decided to place it in the corner of their backyard, where trees provide shade and a stone path leads right up to the front door.

Imagine a playhouse building kit that comes with a pre-assembled floor, walls, and doors. All you have to do is move the parts into place, fasten them together with screws and nails, and you're done. Right? Not so fast. While some kits, like the one pictured here from HomePlace Structures, provide instructions and large, preconstructed parts that help make building go smoothly, the reality is that it will still take more time than you think. Assume a fair amount of trial and error. But with a few extra hands, some basic tools, and a lot of patience, you can expect to erect a playhouse in one weekend.

There are two main types of building kits on the market: modular and precut. The first type provides you with stan-dardized units that fit neatly together, and often come with hardware, flooring, siding, and roofing materials. Instead of building a floor or wall from scratch, you'll simply lift a preassembled piece into place and attach it to other parts of the structure. For families that don't have a lot of time or building know-how, these modular kits must seem very appealing. However, large pre-assembled pieces are typically quite heavy and difficult to maneuver in tight spaces. Although just about all of the materials are provided, you still need a good supply of tools. And even with detailed instructions, a complex project like a playhouse calls for the aid of a carpenter or at least one volunteer with building expertise.

The playhouse on these pages is a miniature log cabin with plenty of real-home amenities. Like many projects built from kits, it's sturdy, weatherproof, and sanded for children's safety. It's also got a quaint porch, three windows, one kid-size front door, and an adult-height back door. Inside, kids can climb up a ladder to a cozy loft space to read quietly or play games. Window boxes welcome visitors with flowers.

Built from a modular kit, this playhouse came with step-by-step instructions and precut pieces that fit neatly together. As with any kit, it's a good idea to assume that the kit may require more people, tools, and time than the instructions estimate. Even if your friends and family members can't help you with the actual construction, they will be an enormous help when it comes time to lift and move the heavier pieces.

For any playhouse, you need a level site. Using tape measure and levels, create a footprint of the cabin floor that approximates the length and width of the foundation. Use this footprint to check for ample distance between the cabin and nearby structures.

The 8-by-12-foot cabin can fit several fun play areas, such as a mini kitchen set, a table, and a couple of chairs.

Tools List

WHAT THEY SAY YOU NEED

- Hammers
- Nail guns, compressor, air hoses
- Tin snips
- Utility knife
- Two stepladders and one plank ladder
- Circular saw
- Tape measure
- Level

WHAT ALSO HELPS GET THE JOB DONE

- Piano dolly
- Multiple screw guns (used instead of nail guns) with extra battery packs
- Pair of clamps
- Gloves
- Safety glasses
- Rubber mallet
- More than one level

Floor

1 MOVE THE FLOOR. With several helping hands, lift the very heavy cabin floor onto a piano dolly and carefully steer it into place.

2 PLACE THE FLOOR ON PRE-GRADED GROUND. According to the manufacturer, the floor can be placed directly on the ground for a cabin of the size shown; larger cabins require a foundation. Be aware that lifting and moving the preassembled cabin pieces can loosen nails and parts, creating a hazard. Inspect pieces for loose or twisted nails that you need to remove or hammer back in.

3 LEVEL THE FLOOR WITH SHIMS. Use levels along the width and length of the floor to gauge the degree of tilt all around. To raise the floor where it is too low, cut and insert pieces of wood, or shims, under the floor beams. To lower it, lift the floor slightly and dig into the dirt underneath. Continue to make adjustments until the floor is level.

Expect the Unexpected

Leave plenty of time to deal with surprises. The large wood floor for this log cabin was damaged during shipping. One beam was cracked in two (right), several joists were wrenched out of place, and other pieces were chipped or broken. The build team repaired everything. To fix the beam, they replaced the broken piece with a new one, which they spliced to the old beam with a 2 × 4 (far right).

Walls

1 **BEGIN WITH THE SIDE WALLS.** Position each wall so the notch in the top corner is toward the front of the cabin. The wall should be flush with the back of the floor, and be sure the paperboard material at the bottom is outside the floor's edge. Clamps come in handy to hold the walls steady as you drill the first screws through the bottom of the wall's framing into the floor.

2 **INSTALL THE FRONT WALL.** Move the wall, with its built-in windows and child-size door, into position, keeping it flush with the two side walls. You may need to gently pull the side walls out a bit to position the front wall. Similarly, have helpers gently push the side walls inward as you attach them to the front wall.

3 **ADD THE BACK WALLS.** Secure one half of the back wall to a side wall (you can start with either side), keeping it flush with the floor. Before attaching the second half, measure the distance between the back-wall modules to make sure that you've left enough room for the rear door's actual width, and that this width matches the opening in the rear gable.

4 **FINISH SECURING THE WALLS TO THE FLOOR AND EACH OTHER.** Finish drilling screws through the bottom 2 × 4s and into the floor. Also drill screws diagonally into the front wall and through the side walls. A distance of about 18 inches between screws should be enough, but a few extra screws in tight corners won't hurt a thing.

Loft

1 **ATTACH THE RAILINGS TO THE STRUCTURE.**
Position the side railings and check that they line up with the center of the side wall's 4 × 4 post (the wall's top notch will allow you to gauge the 4 × 4's width). That way, when you fasten the railing with screws, the screws will go into the 4 by 4. Repeat with the second side railing.

2 **ATTACH THE RAILING TO THE POST.** Stand the front porch posts, which will support the loft, against the railings. Before attaching, measure the distance between the top of the posts and the front wall to make sure it matches the width of the loft. Also measure the distance between the two posts to make sure it matches the length of the loft.

3 **POSITION THE LOFT ON THE POSTS.** Before securing the loft to the posts, make sure all the parts fit. If necessary, remove the loft and move the railings or posts into optimum position. Then attach posts by toe-screwing through the posts and into the floor, and drilling screws through the railings and into the posts.

4 **SECURE THE LOFT.** You'll know right away if side walls are not lined up properly because the notches in them will not line up with the notches in the loft's framing. With a helper or two standing by to keep it steady, attach the loft to the front wall with screws.

Gables and Rafters

1 **LIFT THE FRONT GABLE INTO PLACE.** Inspect the porch posts again and use a mallet to reposition them if necessary. Because the front gable is large and heavy, hold it in place with clamps while you work. Even after you have finished securing the gable to the loft floor, it will be unstable, so you may need to ask a helper to hold it in place until you can temporarily brace it to the loft floor or rafters.

2 **ATTACH THE FRONT GABLE TO THE LOFT.** Screw the front gable through its 2 × 4 framing into the loft. Make sure that the connections between the posts, loft, and gable are the same on each side.

3 **ATTACH THE REAR GABLE.** The rear gable's connection to rear wall pieces is simpler because the module is lighter and the sections are secured to each other via 2 × 4s. Once again, clamps come in handy to keep the gable from moving while you're securing it. Make sure the inside cutout for the door lines up with the insides of the walls below.

4 **MARK FOR RAFTERS.** Although the cabin's instructions indicated there would be markings to show where to attach the rafters, the markings were missing and the build team had to improvise. First they marked the distance between the front gable and the handrail where the loft ends. Then they measured so that the rafters would line up with the roof's plywood panels. They used a square throughout, and repeated the process on the cabin's other side.

Roof

1 **INSTALL THE RAFTERS.** Screw from the top and toe-screw from the sides as needed to give the rafter added stability. With a scrap section of 1 × 3, nail rafters to the front gable to provide temporary support during construction.

2 **SECURE PLYWOOD TO THE RAFTERS.** Starting with the bottom sheet on one side, position the plywood sheathing on the rafters. Measure the space needed for the top sheet (approximately 24 inches), mark it on the rafters, and place the bottom sheet accordingly. Attach with screws. Install the top 2 × 8 plywood piece even with the bottom piece. Secure and repeat on the other side.

3 **ATTACH THE TAR PAPER AND WEATHER STRIP-PING.** Cut a piece of roofing paper that is as long as the length of the roof. Begin stapling the paper onto the roof at the bottom of the roofline. Then put a second piece of paper above the first so that it overlaps at the top (like a big shingle). Once you've papered the entire roof, including the top or peak, nail the aluminum weather stripping around the entire outside edge of the roof, as shown.

4 **BEGIN SHINGLING.** Horizontally overlap the bottom row of shingles to prevent draining water from reaching the roofing paper. To stagger subsequent rows, which do not require horizontal overlapping, move the shingle to the left a bit and trim the excess that hangs over the left edge of the roof. That way, the right seam of the shingle in the second row will not line up with the right seam of the shingle in the first row.

Interior

1 **LEVEL THE FRAMEWORK FOR THE LOFT RAILING.**
The framework consists of a vertical 2 × 2 that runs from the side of the loft alongside a rafter to the plywood ceiling, as well as a horizontal 2 × 2 (the railing's top rail) that runs from this vertical piece to the bottom of a rafter. The loft's framing serves as the railing's bottom rail.

2 **MARK THE RAIL AND THE LOFT FLOOR.** The pickets are precut. Space them 2½ inches apart, then screw them into the top and bottom rails. After the pickets are in place, secure the ladder to the loft and the cabin floor with wood screws.

A cot mattress and throw pillows turn the loft into a private nook for reading or play. A battery or electric lantern adds to the cabin's rustic appeal and sheds light on reading material.

FIT FOR A PRINCESS

NOT EVERY CASTLE NEEDS TO ENDURE THE AGES. THIS PORTABLE STRUCTURE IS EASY TO BUILD AND EVEN EASIER TO TAKE DOWN AND STORE

Isabella, a 3½-year-old who loves to pretend she's living a fairy tale, wished for a castle to enhance her make-believe world. But not a castle in the traditional sense of a fortress. Instead of stone walls, the little girl imagined an inviting tower painted a regal purple. This enchanting and easy-to-assemble playhouse is the result.

Round and octagonal buildings can be tricky to build, but this ingenious structure is quick and straightforward. The roof—the biggest shortcut— is an eight-panel market umbrella, which fits nicely over the building's octagonal shape. The walls consist of plywood trimmed with quarter-round molding to fill the spaces between the panels. The window shutters and doors are cutouts from the walls, adding to the simplicity. Heavy gate hardware adds a medieval touch.

Because it doesn't have a floor, the playhouse is designed for use on a deck or patio. These sorts of spaces usually serve multiple purposes, which is why the building is easy to disassemble and put back up again. The wall sections are held together with door hinges that have removable pins. Taking down the structure is as simple as removing the pins and carrying away the plywood. The entire structure breaks down into one folded-up umbrella plus a stack of plywood 2 feet wide, 5 inches thick, and 5½ feet long.

The walls are 5½ feet high because those proportions seemed to fit Isabella's height. However, this height means that a few inches needed to be cut off the umbrella pole so that the roof rests on the walls. To avoid having to cut off the pole, adjust the wall height to match the pole.

Even the portable containers outside Princess Isabella's door sport crowns.

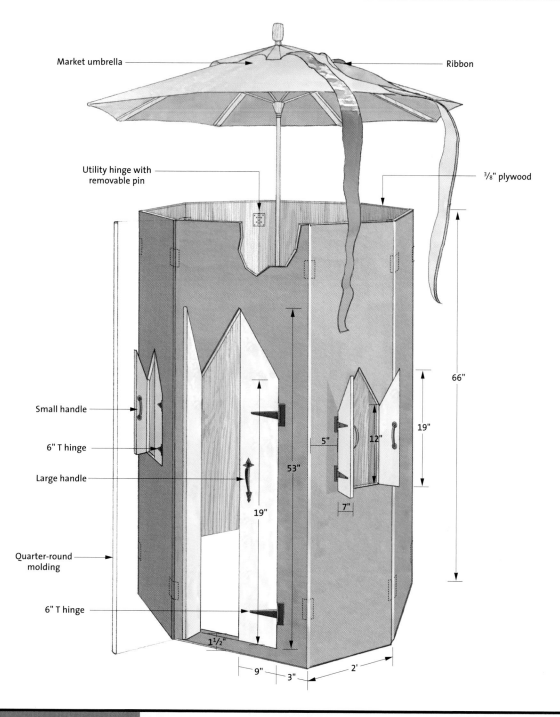

Market umbrella

Ribbon

Utility hinge with removable pin

³/₈" plywood

Small handle

6" T hinge

Large handle

Quarter-round molding

6" T hinge

66"

19"

5"

12"

7"

53"

19"

19"

1½"

9"

3"

2'

Materials List

- Eight-panel 7' market umbrella
- Four sheets ⁵/₈" ACX plywood
- Sixteen 3" utility door hinges with removable pins
- Eight pieces ⁵/₈" quarter round, each 5'4"
- Finish nails, 1¼"

- Four 6" black gate T hinges (for door)
- Eight 4" black gate T hinges (for windows)
- Four black handles (for windows)
- Two black gate handles (for door)
- Paint
- Ribbons or other accessories, as desired

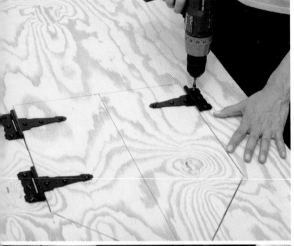

Instructions

Because this playhouse is designed to go on a deck or patio, it needs no other foundation or floor. There is no framing, either. Instead, the walls are cut from ⅝-inch plywood. A good choice is ACX, an exterior plywood with one smooth, knot-free "A" face and one slightly blemished "C" face. (For a uniform look, plan to have all the "A" sides facing either in or out, because the paint takes differently to the smooth side than to the blemished one.) The playhouse requires eight wall panels, each 5½ feet tall and 2 feet wide.

1 **CUT WINDOW AND DOOR OPENINGS.** Create the window shutters and doors at the same time by using a circular saw. Set the blade depth to the thickness of the plywood. Start the cut by tipping the tool backward so that no teeth touch the wood. Turn on the saw and gently lower it into the cut while the blade is spinning. Cut along hinged and peaked edges, but stop short of the corners—you can finish your cuts with a jigsaw.

2 **INSTALL HINGES.** To create perfectly hung shutters or doors with little effort, install hinges before you make the final cuts. Be sure to align the hinges so that the guide on the saw will rest flat on the plywood for all remaining cuts. (Remember to remove the door and window hardware before you paint. Reattach them once the paint dries.)

3 **NUMBER THE PANELS.** Door hinges with removable pins hold the wall sections together. To enable easy reassembly of the panels, even if all hinges aren't at exactly the same height, number the panels before you install the hardware. To keep the project from becoming unwieldy, remove the pins from each pair of panels once hinges are in place. This way, you'll be working with only two panels at a time. The hinges go on the inside of the structure.

4 **PIN SECTIONS.** When all the hinges are in place, pin the wall sections back together in pairs and set them upright. They will stay up on their own. Then couple the pairs together to form the full octagon.

5 **ATTACH MOLDING.** Quarter-round molding fills the gaps between panels in the octagon. Attach the molding with glue and nails. Nail sideways through the molding to pin it to only one wall section. Be sure not to nail into both wall sections or into the space between the panels. Attach molding strips to the same side of each wall section so that every panel winds up with one trim piece.

6 **TRIM THE UMBRELLA.** Set up the umbrella at the center of the playhouse. If there is a gap between the umbrella and the walls, measure it and trim the post by that amount. Or, if the umbrella has a sectional pole, remove the lower part, open the umbrella, and rest it on the walls. Prop the lower part of the pole next to the upper section. The overlapping area should be cut away. Once assembly is complete, paint the walls, doors, and windows.

7 **DECORATE AND ENJOY.** Trimmed with ribbon, the umbrella pole becomes a decorative feature of the playhouse interior. An umbrella support stand is not needed because the umbrella's weight rests on the walls.

8 **STOW AS NEEDED.** When you want to dismantle the playhouse, the pins may be difficult to remove. An easy way to free them is to hammer a slim nail up into the barrel.

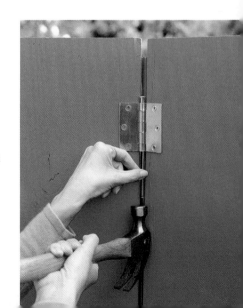

TEEPEES AND CANOPIES

SIMPLE STRUCTURES OFFER AS MUCH EXCITEMENT TO KIDS as more complex play sets. They can hide out, camp under suburban stars, and invent adventures in these spaces. Plus, structures such as teepees and tents can be taken down and stored easily, then reassembled the next day in a different location. Ideal for smaller yards, these structures are best for young children, although larger enclosures that can accommodate older kids are also available.

The soft colors and animal images on this pyramid tent are designed for young campers.

Aidan and Zoey can play camping in this teepee, created with wood poles and washable fabric. On one side it's got a peephole for curious kids. A picnic basket, fake campfire, and real marshmallows complete the picture.

LEFT: A tall bean teepee creates a shady hide-away. Kids can play privately but still be in your sight. ABOVE: A weeping tree is a natural canopy, providing the "structure" children need to escape deep into their imaginations.

A real, more perma-nent teepee blends beautifully into this lush landscape. It also has enough space to welcome older kids and their friends.

NORWEGIAN CABIN

DESIGNED TO BE A PLAYHOUSE NOW AND A POTTING SHED LATER, THIS COTTAGE WITH FLOWERING ROOF WAS INSPIRED BY A FAMILY'S MEMORIES OF SEVERAL YEARS SPENT IN NORWAY

ABOVE: **Lucky pretends she's back in Norway.**
BELOW: **A structure like this can easily be retrofitted to store gardening supplies.**

Like many a quaint Scandinavian outbuilding, this playhouse has a sod roof and a board ceiling. Lucky, the 7-year-old girl for whom this house was built, helped carry and spread the sod, which she sees as a potential habitat for her pet frog. Other homespun details include recycled leaded-glass windows, two of which were kitchen cabinet doors in their original life, and a Dutch door, which was fashioned from an old two-panel door.

It can be tricky to design a kid-size playhouse that has enough headroom for adult use. Several features of this building help to minimize its size while maximizing its space. Bob Stanton, the carpenter who designed and built the structure, skipped the usual roof trusses, allowing the interior to be open all the way up. Instead, the roof is supported by three hefty beams, one at the ridge and two over the side walls. Over those he nailed car decking, 2 × 6 boards with tongue-and-groove edges. Their interlocking design adds strength and stability.

Without trusses, Stanton needed something to pin the walls in place to keep them from bowing out because of the roof load. He stabilized the structure by nailing a few of the roof boards to the top framing piece on the end walls, adding diagonal bracing and mortising studs into the top plate of each side wall. The added joinery gives the structure some of the feel of a timber-frame building, but with cuts that are easy to make.

The roof's peak isn't very high because sod would slide off a steep slope. And, of course, there's all that greenery, which makes the building look like part of the garden—perfect for a playhouse destined to be a potting shed.

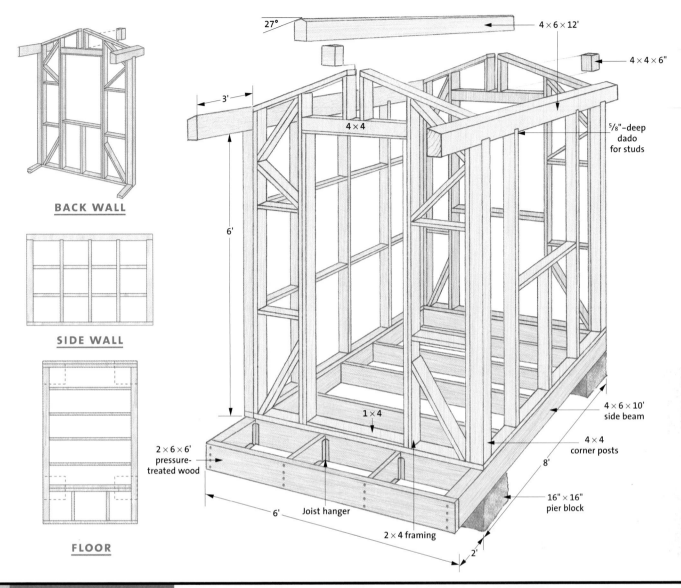

BACK WALL

SIDE WALL

FLOOR

27°

$4 \times 6 \times 12'$

$4 \times 4 \times 6"$

3'

4×4

⅝"–deep dado for studs

6'

$4 \times 6 \times 10'$ side beam

4×4 corner posts

1×4

8'

$2 \times 6 \times 6'$ pressure-treated wood

16" × 16" pier block

6'

Joist hanger

2×4 framing

2'

Materials List

FLOOR

- Four 16" × 16" pier blocks
- Two $4 \times 6 \times 10'$ pressure-treated beams
- Nine $2 \times 6 \times 6'$ pressure-treated joists
- 12 joist hangers for 2 × 6s
- $1\frac{1}{2}$ sheets of ¾" exterior plywood, such as ACX
- Decking material to cover 6' × 2' deck (boards to run in 6' lengths)
- Galvanized nails, 3"

SIDING

- Boards: 27 pieces $1 \times 8 \times 6'$, 14 pieces $1 \times 8 \times 8'$
- Battens: 27 pieces $1 \times 2 \times 6'$, 14 pieces $1 \times 8 \times 8'$
- Corner and trim boards: 11 pieces $1 \times 4 \times 10'$
- Door and jamb
- Windows
- Galvanized siding nails, $2\frac{1}{2}$"
- Galvanized nails for framing, 3"

WALLS

- Framing: 25 pieces $2 \times 4 \times 8'$
- Corners and miscellaneous: two pieces $4 \times 4 \times 12'$, one piece $4 \times 4 \times 6'$
- Windows, as desired

Building Instructions

1 **BUILD THE FLOOR.** The floor consists of four concrete pier blocks recessed into the ground enough so that their top surfaces are level. Joist hangers and nails hold the 4-by-6-inch side beams to the rest of the floor framing. Joists are doubled under end walls of the cabin. The plywood floor (one full sheet and one half sheet cut lengthwise) fits flush with the outside perimeter of the framing.

2 **CUT MORTISES.** Three substantial roof beams add to the traditional feel of this playhouse and allow for the truss-free roof. Cut $\frac{5}{8}$-inch-deep mortises for the side-wall studs. The easiest method is to first make multiple passes with a circular saw, leaving approximately $\frac{1}{8}$ inch between cuts. A chisel quickly cleans out the waste.

3 **BEVEL THE SIDE BEAMS.** The roof's 28-inch rise from side wall to ridge determines the angle of the roof. This photo shows how to cut the side beams so they are beveled to match that slope, since most circular saws don't cut deeply enough to accomplish the job in one pass. Tack a guide piece onto the beam and make the cut shown on the left. Then flip the beam over and cut through the rest of the way to wind up with the piece on the right. If the cuts are not made in this order, you will not have enough wood to support the saw on the final cut.

4 **BUILD THE WALLS.** Frame the walls on the floor to ensure a perfect fit. The side walls run the full length of the floor; the end walls equal the width minus the space needed for the side walls. Because this playhouse will have board-and-batten siding, the framing includes 2-by-4-inch blocking at two heights.

5 **RAISE THE WALLS.** After building the framing for both side walls, nail the board-and-batten siding to the far wall's exterior. To prevent the boards from cracking as they expand and contract due to humidity, leave a nail's width between each board—the batten nails fit into the gaps between the boards, whose edges are held down by the battens. Once the boards and battens are attached, tilt the wall into place. With diagonal bracing holding the wall steady, nail through the bottom plate to secure the wall to the floor; then raise, brace, and nail the other side wall (you can finish the siding for that wall after step 8).

6 **REINFORCE THE ROOF.** There is no framing per se for the roof except along the end walls, where 2 × 4 braces keep the roof weight from pushing the side walls apart.

7 **CUT THE DECKING.** Trim the car decking boards to length and to the roof angle. Instead of doing it piece by piece, line up several planks and cut through them all at once. Car decking is typically sold in 10- or 16-foot lengths, so one setup can yield a dozen of the 5-foot pieces needed for this roof.

8 **BUILD THE ROOF.** After trimming off the groove edge on the end pieces, nail the car decking into place. For most of the pieces, nails go only into the beams. But over the end walls, also nail the car decking to the top brace piece in the wall framing.

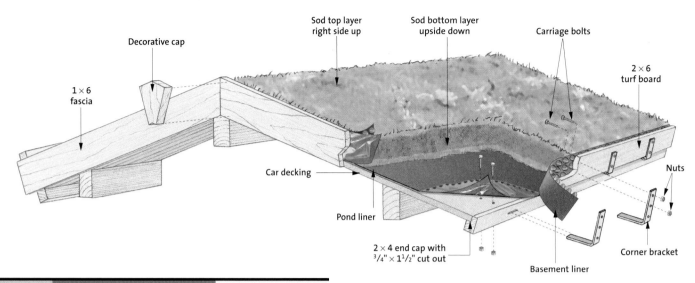

Decorative cap

1 × 6 fascia

Sod top layer right side up

Sod bottom layer upside down

Carriage bolts

2 × 6 turf board

Car decking

Pond liner

Nuts

Corner bracket

2 × 4 end cap with ³/₄" × 1¹/₂" cut out

Basement liner

Materials List

Roof

- Three 4 × 6 × 12' beams
- Fifty-two pieces 2 × 6 × 5' car decking
- Two 2 × 6 × 12' pressure-treated turf boards
- Four 1 × 6 × 6' pressure-treated fascias
- Two 2 × 4 × 12' end caps
- One sheet pond liner, 12' × 14'
- Basement water-channel liner, enough for two panels each 5' × 12'
- Sod, 240 square feet
- Duct tape, 12'
- Eight 6" galvanized corner brackets
- Thirty-two ⁵/₁₆" × 2" carriage bolts with nuts
- Galvanized nails, 2¹/₂"

Installing the Sod Roof

A plastic pond liner big enough to cover the entire roof serves as a waterproof membrane. A dimpled plastic sheet, sold primarily for waterproofing basements (see Resources), is laid over that. Then two layers of turf, one placed grass side down and the other grass side up, are rolled out. The plastic sheet's dimples create an airspace on the back and give the grass roots something to grip on the front. Parallel grooves formed in the plastic point downhill, channeling rainwater off the roof.

1 **CREATE A SLOT TO SET THE GAP.** Drill small side-by-side holes to create a slot for the 6-inch corner brackets, then slip the brackets through (see illustration above). Use a small piece of each of the plastic materials as a spacer for aligning the brackets. Set the gap between the turf board and the roof wide enough to allow both plastic layers to fit underneath.

2 **TACK THE WATERPROOFING.** With the turf board in place, drape the waterproofing layer over the roof and pull up the front and back edges to cover the 1 × 6 fascia pieces on the eaves. To keep the membrane from flopping down, tack it in place along the eaves only. The main roof expanse has no fasteners, so nothing compromises the waterproofing.

3 **INSTALL THE SECOND LAYER.** The basement waterproofing layer comes in a roll. Cut two pieces, one for each side of the roof, and then smooth them in place, positioning them so the grooves run downhill. At the ridge, tape the pieces together with duct tape. At the bottom, push the plastic down so that it extends past the edge of the roof deck and touches the metal brackets. The membrane curls up at the eaves, protecting the wood there.

4 **LAY THE SOD.** Unroll the sod just like carpet. The first layer goes grass side down; the top layer grass side up. Arrange the layers so that joints do not overlap. For the first layer, begin with a piece cut in half crosswise. For the second, start with a piece cut in half lengthwise. Tuck in roots along the edges as you go to avoid a patchwork look.

5 **PLANT IN GAPS.** After a week or two, fill in any gaps with handfuls of soil. Scatter seeds of grass and low-growing wildflowers. If the summers are dry in your area, poke bits of sedum or other succulents into the sod. They will root and spread, allowing the roof to remain green or multicolored (depending on which varieties you select) even during drought. Sod roofs don't need to be mowed, but they may need to be raked every few years to remove excess thatch.

ON THE LOOKOUT

WHETHER KIDS ARE PROTECTING A WILD WEST POST ONE DAY OR HANGING OUT WITH THEIR BUDDIES THE NEXT, THIS STOCKADE WITH LOOKOUT PLATFORM MAKES IT ALL HAPPEN

Roomier than a typical playhouse, this fort also features a watch tower. What's more, it's easy to build. The stockade pieces together almost like a fence, and the lookout is basically a small elevated deck with a roof on top. Because space was tight in this yard, the stockade is just 8 by 8 feet, with a lookout of 4 by 4 feet. Where space allows, the fort can be made larger.

To respect neighbors' privacy, the lookout has solid boards over both back walls. One safety note: The single safety railing is only 2 feet high. If very young children will be using the structure, think about raising the rail and adding vertical pieces between it and the floor. Keep gaps to less than $3\frac{1}{2}$ inches or greater than 9 inches to avoid head entrapment.

Materials List

STOCKADE AND FLAGPOLE

- Posts (includes excess for railing), six $4 \times 4 \times 10'$, one $4 \times 4 \times 12'$, one $4 \times 4 \times 8'$
- Approximately twelve 60-pound bags concrete mix
- Eight rails, $2 \times 4 \times 8'$ (includes gate rails)
- Eighty fence boards, $1 \times 6 \times 6'$ (includes six for gate)
- Galvanized nails, $3\frac{1}{2}"$ and $1\frac{3}{4}"$
- Fence-post cap
- Three screw eyes, $\frac{3}{8}"$
- Rope, 15'
- Caribiner clip
- Pulley
- Cleat

GATE

- Frame pieces, two $2 \times 4 \times 4'$, one $2 \times 4 \times 5'$
- Two 6" T hinges
- Gate latch with string

FLOOR

- Six joists, $2 \times 6 \times 4'$
- Four joist hangers
- Twelve $\frac{1}{2}" \times 5"$ carriage bolts, with lock washers and nuts
- Fourteen decking boards, $2 \times 4 \times 8'$
- Galvanized deck screws, $2\frac{1}{2}"$
- Joist hanger nails

ROOF

- Framing: six $2 \times 4 \times 8'$ (cut to make four pieces 4' long and eight pieces $37\frac{3}{4}"$ long with ends angled 45° with both tips out)
- Ridge beam, $2 \times 6 \times 48"$
- Fourteen fence boards, $1 \times 6 \times 6'$
- Four carriage bolts, $\frac{3}{8}" \times 7"$, with nuts and washers

RAILING

- Two posts, $4 \times 4 \times 2'$ (use excess from stockade posts)
- Rails, one $2 \times 4 \times 4'$, two $2 \times 4 \times 16"$
- Four carriage bolts, $\frac{1}{2}" \times 5"$, with nuts and washers

LADDER

- Three pieces $2 \times 4 \times 8'$, cut into two stringers 67" long, four treads 13" long, and eight tread supports 9" long with ends angled 15°
- Galvanized deck screws, $2\frac{1}{2}"$
- Two galvanized carriage bolts, $\frac{1}{2}" \times 5"$, with nuts and lock washers

PEEPHOLE

- Threaded rod, 8–32, 12" long
- Two cap nuts, 8–32
- Two no. 8 lock washers
- Machine screw nut, 8–32

The stockade that encloses this lookout platform is itself enclosed by the backyard fence. In the lucky situation where playmates are just over the fence, install a second ladder or a clothesline mail-delivery system out the back.

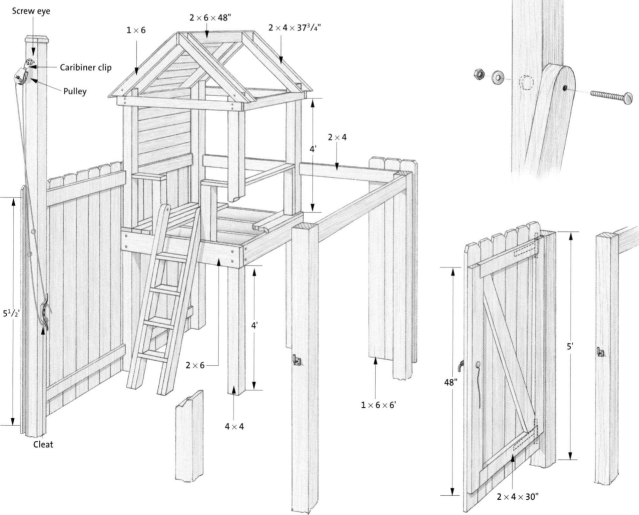

Screw eye

Caribiner clip

Pulley

1 × 6

2 × 6 × 48"

2 × 4 × 37³/₄"

2 × 4

4'

4'

4'

2 × 6

5¹/₂'

Cleat

4 × 4

1 × 6 × 6'

48"

5'

2 × 4 × 30"

Building Instructions

1 **BEGIN WITH THE FLAG.** A little advance planning helps this play structure go together more smoothly. While the first step might seem like it should be done at the end, doing it now eliminates a top-of-the-ladder job later. Install hardware for the flagpole while the post is still flat on the ground. Standard flagpole pulleys attach directly to the post. Or, as shown here, use a screw eye, a caribiner clip, a standard pulley, and a decorative fence-post cap.

2 **INSTALL THE POSTS.** Set the posts as described on page 41 after determining the width needed for the gate: the width of six fence boards plus ½ to ¾ inch of swing space plus whatever gap is needed for the hinges. When the posts are in place, notch into the two that are at the back of the fort at the height of the floor of the lookout (4 feet). The joist there needs to fit into these grooves to put the back walls of the fort on the same plane as the fence boards around the stockade. To cut the grooves, make multiple passes with a circular saw. Chisel out the waste.

3 **BUILD THE RAILS.** Toenail the fence rails in place with 3½-inch galvanized nails. To keep the rails aligned while driving the nails at an angle, tack or clamp a block of scrap wood underneath.

4 **ASSEMBLE FLOOR AND ROOF.** Floor joists are held in place with metal hangers. Special hanger nails have the thickness needed for strength but are short enough not to go through 2 × lumber. When the lookout framing is done, nail on the floor and then stand on it to build the roof. To create a base for the roof, nail four 4-foot 2 × 4s horizontally to the posts 4 feet above the floor. Nail rafters in pairs to this base along the side walls and to the ridge beam. Two pairs of rafters go on the outside of the main posts and two go on the inside. Lock the assembly in place by threading a 7-inch carriage bolt through the post and the two rafters at each corner.

5 **REINFORCE THE LADDER.** A sturdy ladder has treads supported by wood, not just nails or screws. Either cut grooves at an angle that will allow the treads to sit flat, using a procedure similar to that for cutting grooves in the posts in step 2, or, as shown here, cut angled supports and fit them against the ladder rails between each tread. Screw the parts together.

6 **FRAME THE GATE.** The gate's top and bottom rails are notched into the side framing pieces, and a diagonal brace prevents sagging. The brace, which must fit precisely, runs from the top on the latch side to the bottom on the hinge side.

7 **ATTACH HINGES.** Because of their T shape, the gate's hinges need to be aligned with the top and bottom rails of the framing. The easiest way to hang a gate is while it consists of just the frame and the board or two that will fit under the hinge. The rest of the boards can be nailed on while the gate is in place.

8 **CUT A PEEPHOLE.** For a fun detail, create a 2-inch-wide peephole with a doorknob hole saw. Cut out a 3-inch circular cover with a jigsaw. Swing the cover back and forth over the hole to locate the best position for a pivot. Then drill a 3/16-inch hole through the cover and the fence. Screw a cap nut and a lock washer onto one end of the threaded rod and insert it through the fence board. Add another lock washer. The peephole cover and the other cap nut complete the setup. Make sure the cover swings freely so that it closes on its own.

KIDS ON DECK

BUILDING A PLATFORM OR DECK IN YOUR BACKYARD can produce a dramatic effect by instantly giving definition to an outdoor space. A low platform or deck, which is simpler to build than one that stands on posts, is sometimes all a child needs to stage a variety of adventures. Happily, this same platform can serve you, too. Set up chairs and a table on one end for entertaining or dining and let the kids frolic on the other.

Concrete pier

Beam

12"   5'

End joist

Constructing Without Posts

Deck construction may seem like a daunting task, especially ones that are built on top of posts set in the ground or on concrete footings. But a low-level deck can simply rest on precast concrete piers or on pressure-treated 4 × 6s that are lying directly on the ground. This type of deck provides all of the benefits of elevated platforms, with a lot less work. Basic materials include lumber, precast concrete piers, and hardware. If your backyard slopes, you can install posts below the deck at its low end; the beams can rest directly on piers at the high end.

To build a low deck with no posts, install at least two rows of piers (more for a larger deck) to support identical beams along each row. Construct the beams of 2 × 8s that have been nailed together. The inside board should be shorter by 1½ inches at both ends, to create a place for the end joist to fit (see illustration at left). Attach the beam to the pier with a post cap, and the joists to the inside faces of each beam with joist hangers.

This freestanding cedar deck is blessed with a woodsy setting and dappled shade. Casual furniture creates an inviting outdoor room, ideal for conversation and just spacious enough for a dancing child or two. Note the planters on the railing.

A Deck Without Footings

Small platform decks like the one shown at right require no poured concrete and do not even use precast piers. The foundation can consist of two 4 × 6 timbers partially buried belowground. Timbers used this way must be pressure treated and rated for ground contact. Joists rest on top of the timbers.

Dig two parallel trenches that are about 6 inches deep for the timbers, then add about 4 inches of sand to each trench. Set the timbers on the sand as shown below and make sure they are perfectly parallel. Level the timbers by adding or removing sand, then fill in the trenches by adding sand to the sides of the timbers.

Mark a joist layout on each timber. Install the joists on top of the timbers with two 12d toe-nails or two 2½–inch deck screws driven at an angle through each side into the beam. Trim the joist ends, if necessary, and attach the rim joists. Install the decking.

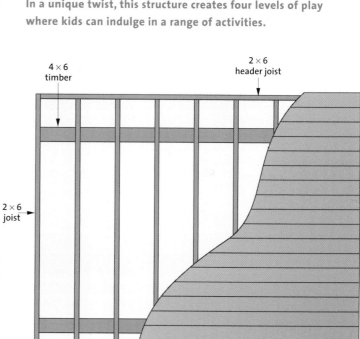

In a unique twist, this structure creates four levels of play where kids can indulge in a range of activities.

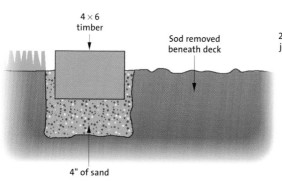

4 × 6 timber

Sod removed beneath deck

4" of sand

4 × 6 timber

2 × 6 header joist

2 × 6 joist

2 × 6 decking

Multiple Uses for Low Decks

FOR KIDS	FOR YOU
A platform for jumping on and off	A platform for outdoor dining
A stage for pretend play or theater	A stage for hosting events
A retreat for reading or drawing	A retreat for sunbathing
A floor for a kid-size picnic table	A floor for patio furnishings

QUICK, SIMPLE TREE HOUSE

IN JUST ONE WEEKEND, A FATHER HAM-
MERED TOGETHER THIS TREE HOUSE
FOR HIS KIDS. A LITTLE SERENDIPITY AND
A BIT OF COMMON SENSE PLANNING
STREAMLINED THE WORK

Materials List

For a tree house approximately 5' × 6':

SUPPORT

- Four trees or a combination of trees
  and posts 4 × 4 × 10$^{1}/_{2}$'
- Concrete or gravel for post holes,
  as needed
- Galvanized nails, 2$^{1}/_{2}$" and 3"

DECK

- Supports: five 2 × 8 × 6', two 2 × 8 × 5'
- Fourteen floor boards, 2 × 6 × 5'

ROOF

- Beams: two 2 × 6 × 5', three 2 × 6 × 6'
- Framing: two 2 × 4 × 3',
  four 2 × 4 × 4$^{1}/_{2}$'
- Fourteen cedar boards, $^{5}/_{4}$" × 12 × 4$^{1}/_{2}$'

RAILING

- Eight pieces 2 × 4 × 8', cut as needed
- Trim pieces: four 1 × 3 × 6',
  two 1 × 3 × 5', two 1 × 3 × 2$^{1}/_{2}$'
- 8" bevel cedar siding: eight 6',
  four 5', four 2$^{1}/_{2}$' (approximately
  80 linear feet)

STAIRS

- Two 2 × 10 stringers, with ends
  angled 75°
- Five treads, 2 × 6 × 2'

Luck was on Bryan Johnson's side when he found three slender conifers spaced conveniently 5 to 6 feet apart. Choosing this site meant he'd only have to add one 4 × 4 post to serve as the fourth corner post for his kids' tree house.

Planning to build the tree house only 4 feet off the ground also helped speed construction along, freeing Bryan from needing a ladder for most of the work. He only did some minor tweaking to the pole-framing technique described on page 33,

but he skipped a step: building walls. Instead, he erected what is essentially a deck supported by the three trees and the post. Then, higher up on the same supports, he built a roof. The floor and the roof float independently, yet constitute a complete tree house, because Bryan filled in the railings with siding boards.

Bryan didn't worry about making the floor exactly square. When he got to the roof, however, he needed a nearly perfect rectangle to make the ⁵⁄₄-by-12 cedar roofing boards line up properly. Two of the trees wound up inside the roofline, so Bryan cut into a few roof boards to accommodate their trunks. He added no other roofing, figuring that rain would blow in through the sides of the structure anyway.

While Bryan made just a small investment in both time and money, the play value was great. Though perfectly safe, the tree house is deliberately not designed to last forever or withstand the pressures that the trees will exert on it as they grow—they could eventually squeeze the building, causing the floor or roof to buckle. Bryan, however, expects the tree house will last at least as long as his kids stay interested in it.

OPPOSITE: **A pulley and rope make a neat delivery system for mail, supplies, and even larger items.**

2×6

$^5\!/_4 \times 12$

2×4

2×4

2×6

2×4

4×4

2×6

1×3

Bevel siding

2×8

2×10

A Tree House Built by Pros

A LICENSED CONTRACTOR CAN BUILD A STURDY, LONG-LASTING STRUCTURE, BUT IT TAKES THE VISION OF A KID TO CREATE A TREE HOUSE AS NICE AS THIS

Eric and a friend take in the view from his professionally built tree house.

Nine-year-old Eric had a dream for his tree house: It would be a medieval-looking structure, with tall, thin windows flanking a heavy door with iron hardware. Over the center of the roof there would be a lookout tower for spying on kids using a neighborhood trail. And the entire enterprise would rest in the trees. Eric put his dreams on paper, sketching his vision in as much detail as he could. The TreeHouse Workshop, a company that specializes in treetop retreats, transformed his sketches into plans.

Although super-sturdy and constructed to last for years, this tree house is simple enough for people who relish challenging weekend projects, such as building a deck or a potting shed, to do. Because no two trees are the same, it's unlikely that you will be able to copy this plan exactly. But the basic steps—and solutions—will work for most tree house projects.

The first hurdle is to decide which tree or trees to use. For this project, Eric's family favored two towering Douglas firs, one with two trunks, about 12 feet from their back deck. The tree house would be 8 feet off the ground, on the high side of a slope. Locating the tree house here turned out to be a brilliant move, because the easy access encourages frequent use.

Some branches were dead, though, and sap oozed from one trunk. So they did what anyone contemplating a hefty tree house would be wise to do: They called in an arborist, who removed the dead branches and thinned the live ones to lessen the wind pressure against the trees and tree house.

One lesson they learned from hindsight: Prune a season in advance, especially in springtime, to minimize the dripping of sap onto your tree house.

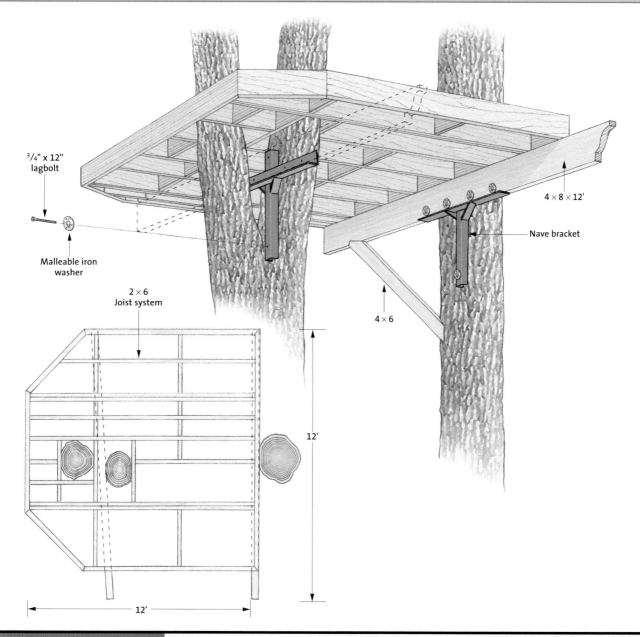

¾" x 12" lagbolt

Malleable iron washer

2 × 6 Joist system

12'

12'

4 × 8 × 12'

Nave bracket

4 × 6

Materials List

FOR A DECK APPROXIMATELY 12' × 12':

- Two nave brackets (see details in step 2)
- One 2 × 4 × 40" for nave bracket template
- Six galvanized lag bolts, ¾" × 12"
- Eight galvanized bolts, ⅝" × 5", with nuts and malleable iron washers
- Two Douglas fir beams, 4 × 8 × 12'
- Two braces, 4 × 6 × 10'
- Douglas fir joists, thirteen 2 × 6 × 12', two 2 × 6 × 8'
- Twenty-five pieces of pressure-treated decking, 2 × 6 × 12'

- Deck screws, 3" (20 pounds of screws were used for the tree house, bridge, and lookout)

FOR THE DECK TRIM AND RAILING:

- Four cedar boards, 1 × 8 × 12'
- Four cedar planks, 2 × 6 × 12'
- Eight cedar pieces, 2 × 4 × 12'
- Ten posts, 4 × 4 × 8'
- Approximately 125 sturdy branches, each 30½" long and at least 1½" in diameter

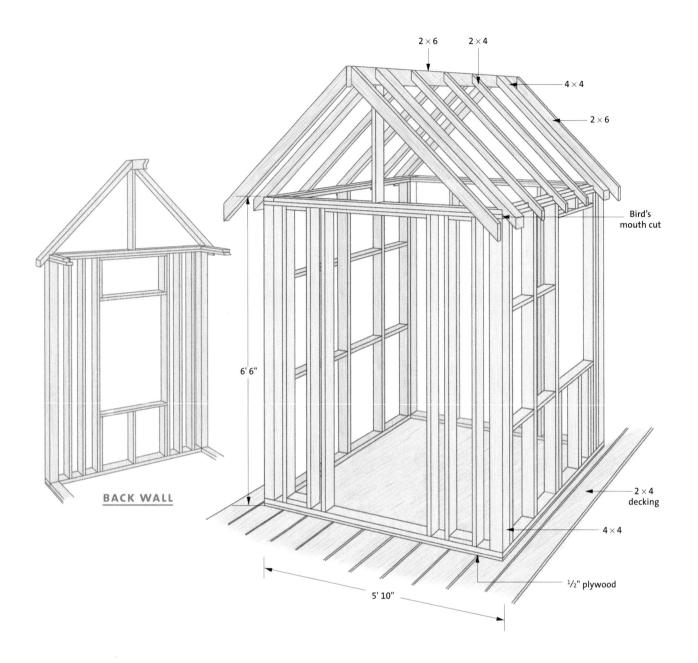

2 × 6   2 × 4

4 × 4

2 × 6

Bird's
mouth cut

2 × 4
decking

4 × 4

½" plywood

6' 6"

5' 10"

BACK WALL

Materials List

FOR A TREE HOUSE APPROXIMATELY 6' × 6':

- Studs: eight 2 × 4 × 14', seven 2 × 4 × 12', five 2 × 4 × 10'
- Framing pieces: one 2 × 6 × 8', two 4 × 4 × 10', two 4 × 4 × 14'
- Twenty-two exterior boards: eight 1 × 10 × 14', fourteen 1 × 10 × 8'
- Cedar battens, 1" × 2", same lengths as boards
- Three and a half sheets of ½" exterior plywood
- Metal roofing to cover two sides, each approximately 4' × 7', with roofing screws and ridge cap

This project used recycled windows and an old door cut down to 2 by 6 feet. The materials listed here are what's needed for a tree house with just that door opening. For each window you add, you will probably need two or three additional 2 × 4s. Adding these will reduce the number of board-and-batten pieces you need.

The Key Component

The biggest issue in building a tree house is attaching it to the tree or trees so the house stays up and the structure doesn't damage the nutrient-carrying layer under the bark with excessive rubbing. Although it may sound complicated, the easiest way to accomplish both goals is to order custom T-shape supports from a metal fabricator or welding shop. The TreeHouse Workshop refers to these pieces as "nave brackets" because their shape follows the floor plan of medieval cathedrals in Europe. This tree house needed two supports, which cost about $100 each.

1 **NAVE BRACKET.** To make a template for the nave-bracket fabricator, strap a 40-inch-long 2 × 4 along the central axis of the trunk. Then level and screw on a 2 × 4 crosspiece at the height of the lowest edge of the tree house deck structure. This produces a template adjusted for the tree's slant.

2 **INSPECT THE BRACKET.** The vertical piece is a 40-inch length of 3-inch steel channel ($^3/_{16}$ inch thick). The crosspiece is a 48-inch length of 3-inch angle iron (also $^3/_{16}$ inch thick). These pieces are welded into a cross, arranged so that the upper section does not project beyond the height of the deck. Steel triangles welded to the main pieces provide reinforcement. A $^3/_4$-inch hole at each end of the vertical piece and four holes along the crosspiece allow the fitting to be bolted to the tree and to the deck supports.

Building the Support Structure

Using the special metal supports and staying within ladder height of the ground makes it possible to put the tree house's support structure together almost like you would a deck. A two- or three-person crew speeds the work and reduces the number of trips up and down a ladder. Building a support structure is not a job for children, however. Take care to keep them out of the path of any objects that might fall.

1 **DRILL PILOT HOLES.** After establishing one tree as a reference point, trap a nave bracket into place and drill pilot holes for the two ³⁄₄-inch galvanized lag bolts that will tie the metal to the tree. Use a long auger bit in a half-inch drill equipped with handles, a professional setup available from tool-rental companies. Or, to do the job using typical homeowner-scale tools, drill down as far as possible with a spade bit, then add a bit extension and continue drilling to the depth needed for the bolts.

2 **ESTABLISH THE POSITION OF THE SECOND NAVE BRACKET.** Strap a 2 × 4 to the bottom of the first bracket and extend the wood to the other tree. Using a level, fine-tune the 2 × 4's position, then temporarily screw it into place. Repeat this process with a second 2 × 4 on the other side of the trees. Then, with a helper or two, hoist the second nave bracket and bolt it into place.

3 **BOLT BEAMS TO BRACKETS.** With both nave brackets attached, bolt on one of the 4 × 8 support beams. The shelf created by the angle iron makes this step easy as long as all the holes line up properly. The malleable iron washers (see Resources) provide more bearing surface than ordinary flat washers and look fancier.

4 **FRAME THE DECK.** The deck rim, made of 2 × 6 Douglas fir, comes next. Instead of nailing the framing into place, use 3-inch ceramic-coated deck screws (see Resources). When you're working on a ladder, a drill gives you more control than a hammer does, and parts stay aligned better.

5 **BRACE FRAMING TO TREES.** Before adding the rest of the framing, install two diagonal braces to help shift the tree house's weight back to the trees. Figuring out where to cut the braces is tricky because the top must be inset slightly into the beam, while the base needs to fit perfectly flush with the bark. To create a template for the top cut, snap a chalk line onto stiff paper and then copy the shape onto the beam.

6 **BOLT BRACE TO TREES.** The lower edge of the diagonal brace requires only a simple angle cut and perhaps a little judicious paring of the bark so there's a flat place for the end to rest. Shallow cuts into a small section of bark won't harm the tree. To keep the tree's moisture from wicking into the brace, slip a piece of mudsill gasket material into the joint and then attach the brace to the tree with a 12-inch galvanized lag bolt.

Building the Deck and the Tree House

Once you've built the support structure, the job proceeds much like any deck-construction project, then shifts to steps similar to those for building a garden shed. There are a few differences, however. Because this deck also supports the tree house, you need to size the joists according to flooring span charts, not those generated for decks. And, of course, the tree house is located up in the air. Plan the work so that you can stand on the ground or on the platform whenever possible. Working on a ladder is not only more dangerous, it's also more time-consuming and harder on your body.

1 **INSTALL THE FLOOR.** After installing a network of 2 × 6 joists spaced approximately 16 inches apart, screw on 2 × 6 deck boards. These will serve as flooring for the outdoor areas and as a subfloor for the interior.

2 **GLUE INTERIOR SUBFLOOR.** A liberal zigzag of construction adhesive around the perimeter of the floor, and at regular spots in the middle, seals the plywood floor to the decking and keeps rainwater out. The decking alone would be strong enough for a tree house floor, but the addition of plywood allows for interior carpeting, a feature Eric hoped for.

3 **FRAME THE WALLS.** Frame the first wall on the ground and then lift it onto the platform, where you can install the window. It's easiest to build everything on the ground, but the weight can become too much for a few people to lift without the help of pulleys and ropes. Doing the work partly on the ground and partly on the platform proved easiest in this case.

4 **ATTACH THE SIDING.** The tree house's two side walls nearly abut the trees. Here the board-and-batten siding and exterior window trim were installed before the walls were fixed in place.

5 **RAISE THE RAFTERS.** After nailing a king post to the top of each gabled wall, hoist the ridge beam into place on top of the post and nail on the rafters. Notches in the rafters provide secure footing against the top plate. Using metal rafter ties instead would simplify this step.

6 **BUILD THE RAILS.** For the railing, the family used some of the branches trimmed from the fir trees and supplemented them with cedar branches, also from their property. Because branches are rarely straight, the TreeHouse Workshop crew built a jig that allows each piece to settle into its natural alignment. The jig also makes it easy to cut each piece exactly to length. A screw through each end secures the pieces to the railing framing. For a sturdy railing, use only sound branches that are at least 1¹/₂ inches in diameter and space them 3 inches apart.

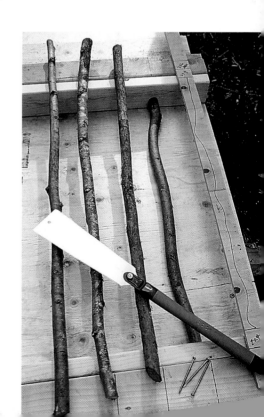

ABOVE: **The crow's nest perches on four thick bolts and malleable iron washers, available at industrial-supply companies. The bolts provide a perch, and the washers create a lip that keeps the tree house from sliding.**

RIGHT: **Eric's crow's nest rises over the deck of his tree house. The deck acts as a safety feature, keeping a child from falling all the way to the ground.**

BELOW: **The trapdoor, about 2 feet square, opens in the middle. Holes cut into two of the decking boards serve as handles.**

A Crow's Nest Lookout

For spying on people using a trail below or for launching pinecones against "the enemy," the best spot in the neighborhood is this crow's nest, which fits right between the double trunks of a towering Douglas fir. Although it was built as an add-on to the tree house featured on the previous pages, a project such as this could also serve as a small stand-alone tree house.

Instead of using the custom steel brackets that support the tree house, this overlook is attached to the tree with four 1-inch-wide galvanized lag bolts 12 inches long. The bolts are screwed only partway into the tree, allowing the excess to provide a perch for the floor framing. Malleable iron washers serve as stops that lock the platform into place. One critical detail is that the bolts must be long enough to penetrate solid wood, not just bark.

Framing for the floor consists of 4 × 8 beams half-lapped where they intersect. The ladder leads to a trapdoor in the floor, a cool detail that saves space.

RIGHT: **Eric tests out the clatter bridge.**

BELOW: **The bridge rests on two thick galvanized chains. Carriage bolts ¹/₂ inch thick thread through the links to secure the 2 × 12 planks. Bolts through the links also secure the chains to framing at either end of the bridge.**

BOTTOM: **The builders used pressure-treated 4 × 4s set into concrete to anchor the bridge at the deck end. To hide the incised wood, they boxed over it with beveled cedar boards to create a sleeve.**

A Clatter-Bridge Entry

Although a simple ladder works fine as a way to get up and down from a tree house, a clatter bridge adds tremendously to the fun.

Kids use this bridge, which links the tree house to the family's deck 12 feet away, to launch water balloons on passersby and tie bird netting to it to see what they can catch. And, of course, children running on a clatter bridge generate a lot of noise.

A bridge such as this must start and end at approximately the same level. To get up to the level of the tree house floor, as well as clear the rail around the family's deck, the builders installed a ladder at one end of the bridge. Diagonal braces serve as a handrail for the ladder and also bolster the bridge's support posts, which are set into concrete. Cutouts in the decking allow the diagonal braces to run underneath the deck and tie into its support structure. On the tree house end, the chains pass through holes in the rim joist of the deck and are bolted to the next joist. Given all the bouncing that's likely to occur, strong connections at both ends are very important.

Manila rope 1¹/₂ inches thick serves as a handrail on the bridge. Because the bridge isn't very high and because the children who play here are well past the toddler stage, the family elected not to fill in the space under the rope. If you desire more security, one solution is to string a second rope low down and then weave it diagonally to create netting.

swings 'n' things

A GREAT PLAY SET TESTS KIDS' PHYSICAL LIMITS WITH A MIX
OF FUN FEATURES. COMPLEX STRUCTURES THAT ALLOW FOR
ACCESSORIES AND ADD-ONS WILL ENTERTAIN AND ENGAGE
THEM FOR YEARS. IN THIS CHAPTER WE SHOW YOU HOW
TO PLAN AND BUILD SEVERAL SWING SETS, AS WELL AS HELP
YOU TIE A BOWLINE FOR A SAFE TIRE SWING.

SAFETY CONSIDERATIONS

Pea gravel provides cushioning for the kids who get to play on this backyard structure.

CUTS AND BRUISES ARE A RITE OF CHILDHOOD. But more serious injuries can occasionally occur, even in the backyard. To minimize risks, steer children toward age-appropriate activities and demonstrate how to use equipment properly. Even with the best planning and materials, you or another adult should supervise toddlers and pre-schoolers. As kids get older and more mature, your level of supervision will change, too. Here are some recommendations.

Lay Out Safety Zones

● SLIDES. Allow 6 feet of clearance in all directions. From the bottom of the slide, measure a safety zone equal to the height of the slide plus 4 feet. However, slides taller than 10 feet don't need a landing zone greater than 14 feet.

● STANDARD SWINGS. Because children may jump from a swing while it's in motion, the safety zone in front and back must be twice the height of the swing from the pivot point.

● TIRE SWINGS. The safety zone is a circle with a radius equal to the chain or rope height plus 6 feet. Also plan a 6-foot safety zone around the swing's supporting structure, since kids are apt to climb this as well.

Provide Adequate Cushioning

Grass and soil may be fine for most of the yard, but they may not provide enough padding under play sets. Safety experts recommend installing a thick layer of shock-absorbent material under and around swings, slides, and other equipment. The chart on the opposite page provides details on some commonly used materials. Sand and wood mulch are inexpensive mainstays, but newer materials such as rubber mulch and tile products offer better cushioning and easier maintenance. Some manufacturers provide their own versions of these materials, so be sure to ask plenty of questions before buying. And remember, all surfaces require drainage.

A slide ends in a sandbox, softening the landing.

Add Protective Barriers

Railings keep children from falling from tree houses, walkways, and other elevated surfaces. Safety experts recommend installing a railing if the platform is more than 20 inches high for preschoolers and 30 inches for older children. The top surface of a railing should be at least 29 inches above the platform for preschoolers, and 38 inches for older children. A gap between the lower edge of a railing and the platform allows older kids to decide whether they want to scoot under the railing or use another method of getting on and off the structure, but the gap should be less than 3½ inches or greater than 9 inches to avoid head entrapment. For the same reason, also limit the space between uprights to less than 4 inches (although some codes allow 6 inches). These safety standards don't account for helmets, so teach children to remove headgear before they use the equipment.

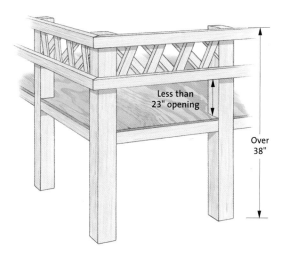

Less than 23" opening

Over 38"

Soft Landings

MATERIAL	COST	CUSHIONING	MAINTENANCE	CONS
Sand and pea gravel	Low	Good at appropriate depth, but compacts in rain and cold weather.	Requires continuous leveling, sifting, and periodic breakup of compacted sand or gravel.	Sand is easily tracked indoors and attracts animals. Gravel is hard to walk on and becomes compacted.
Wood chips and wood mulch	Low	Good at appropriate depth, but compacts with use and exposure.	Requires periodic replacement and continuous leveling and sifting to remove dirt.	Decomposes with time, susceptible to microbial growth when wet, and may conceal trash.
Shredded tires and rubber mulch	Moderate	Superior; does not deteriorate or become compacted.	Requires some leveling and sifting.	Lacks natural appearance. Can be flammable.
Rubber over foam mats or tiles	High	Good, uniform.	Minimal cleaning required.	Undersurfaces may require professional installation. Tiles may curl, causing tripping.

PLAY SETS 101

A PLAY SET BOOSTS BACKYARD FUN and provides kids a space for hours of exercise. While a simple swing set may be all your children need, many structures combine decks, forts, climbing features, and all varieties of slides and swings.

Plan the ideal structure by observing how your children play and anticipating how their play will evolve over the years—and, of course, ask them what they want. Young children will get plenty of action out of a basic set with two swings and a slide.

If your yard regularly attracts groups of children or you have older kids, a large, more complex play structure may be a worthwhile investment. No matter what size yard you have, it's wise to purchase versatile structures that you can update with more-challenging features as kids develop and mature.

A basic swing set with no other attachments is relatively easy to construct and cheap. Yet it provides kids with plenty of play value.

Bringing It Home

To zero in on the best play set for your family, research the various options available at lumberyards, home improvement stores, and specialty dealers. For the youngest children, molded plastic playhouses offer slides and holes to crawl through. These pint-size activity gyms come with parts that lock together and can be easily transported.

With older kids, opt for larger metal or wood structures. Any metal structure should be made of heavy-gauge steel, galvanized or painted to prevent rust. The sturdiest and most attractive structures are made of wood, most commonly cedar and redwood, which are naturally rot-resistant, or other pressure-treated varieties. Play-set swings, slides, and other parts are usually composed of durable metal, plastic, or vinyl materials.

In terms of play-set types and costs, you have three basic choices:

● Do it yourself. Lumberyards and home improvement stores sell all of the basic hardware and lumber to complete projects like the ones in this book. They also sell kits with plans. In both cases, you do all the cutting, drilling, smoothing, and staining, but the process is spelled out for you.

Figure on more time for assembly than plans estimate, however.

The kit's price doesn't usually include the lumber, but the sales staff should be able to estimate the price of wood and other components. Features such as swings, slides, and hardware may be sold individually. Altogether, the plan, hardware, and lumber for an entry-level swing set with a fort and slide generally costs $750 and up.

● PRECUT PLANS AND PARTS. Companies that specialize in play sets sell kits with all the necessary parts, including precut lumber. The amount of prep work varies. In some kits, the wood is simply cut to length, drilled for bolts, and stained. In others, every edge is rounded and every bolt hole is countersunk—jobs that can take a while even with the best tools. Some factories preassemble other parts, such as railings and floor panels, saving you time. But you still need to follow detailed instructions—and expect a few surprises.

Stores that specialize in play sets generally encourage customers to pick and choose the features they want. These stores may also send a designer to your home to determine the best configuration for your yard. Plan on spending anywhere from $1,500 to $5,000 for a kit that includes precut lumber. Add a few hundred dollars if you opt for professional assembly.

● CUSTOM DESIGN. If you design and build the play structure yourself, it doesn't need to cost any more than one of similar size assembled from a lumber-yard kit. You and your kids get exactly what you want. But doing it on your own will probably take longer at every step, from finalizing the plan to buying parts to building the structure.

The other way to get a custom design is to hire someone to create it. Garden shows sometimes feature companies that specialize in this craft. Some deck builders and general contractors can also build play sets. A sketch or a model is often enough to give a builder an idea of what you want. Depending on the complexity of the structure, the size, and the materials, prices range from a few hundred to tens of thousands of dollars.

Adding Accessories

The simplest way to keep a play structure fresh and exciting is to get one with multiple built-in accessories, such as large swing-and-slide sets. Companies that specialize in play structures often offer add-ons or accessories designed to go with their products, which you can add anytime. Examples include slides, rope ladders, fireman's poles, rock-climbing walls, monkey bars, deck roofs, lower floors and walls, and bridges and connecting towers.

If the dealer from which you purchase a play set does not offer add-ons, you can sometimes buy them separately from a home improvement store. You'll find a wide variety of swings (belt, bucket, disk, and glider styles) and slides sold this way. Make sure that the add-on is not designed to fit only a specific brand and that it will not affect your set's structural integrity.

SELECTING A PLAY SET

THERE'S AN ENDLESS VARIETY OF PLAY SET STYLES, sizes, and colors on the market. Before you decide on one, shop around and think through what will best suit your yard as well as your children's interests and abilities. Then be sure to ask a lot of questions about the materials and components to get the best value. Use the checklist on the following page to help you make your selection.

Backyard play sets can offer as much to your kids as the ones they enjoy at the playground. In addition to tire swings and climbing features, consider fun extras like flags and binoculars (top right). Custom play sets (bottom) often use vivid colors and a sort of fantasy-fortress look to draw kids in.

Play Set Checklist

Whether you're eyeing ready-made play sets or shopping for parts to build one yourself, you'll find a range of options for every component. Here's a checklist of issues to consider.

WOOD

☐ Is the wood pressure-treated?

☐ How hefty are the pieces? Look for 4 × 4 posts, 4 × 4 swing beams, and ³/₄-inch deck boards.

☐ Are edges smoothed and corners rounded, especially on railings and platforms?

HARDWARE

☐ Is the hardware residential or commercial rated? Residential swing hangers must carry 160 pounds on two chains. Commercial ones hold 5,000 pounds.

☐ How many lag bolts are there, and are holes drilled for them?

☐ Does metal rub against metal in key spots, such as swing hangers? Hangers with nylon bushings last longer. Bronze bearings lubricated by oil sealed into the fitting are even better.

☐ Are S hooks used to fasten chains or ropes? S hooks can pinch skin and catch clothing if they are only partially bent shut.

ROPES AND CHAINS

☐ How heavy are they, and what load are they designed to carry?

☐ Is the chain coated? Plastic film reduces the chance of pinched fingers.

☐ Polyester rope is softer to touch, less stretchy, and more sun-resistant than nylon.

☐ Does rope present a safety hazard? There is no risk of strangulation if both ends are fastened and the slack allows only a 5-inch circle to be formed.

STABILITY

☐ Which age range is specified on the play set? A set described as suitable for children ages 2 to 5 may tip if older children use it.

☐ Do metal braces and bolts with nuts (not just lag bolts) fortify key joints, such as those between the swing beam and the play set's legs? Connections that rely only on nails or screws are weak.

☐ Is the structure designed so that legs or braces form triangle shapes?

SWINGS

☐ How high is the swing beam? The higher the beam, the larger the area of safety surfacing you need.

☐ Are single-axis and multiple-axis swings separated?

☐ Are swing seats made of soft and flexible plastic or rubber? These are safer than those made of hard materials such as wood or metal.

☐ What is the spacing between swings? The minimum residential standard is 8 inches between swings.

SLIDES

☐ How much do you want one? Preschoolers love slides, but the attraction often fades around kindergarten age.

☐ How is the slide constructed? Single-wall slides often need to have 2 × 4s bolted down the sides for stiffening.

A TYPICAL ASSEMBLY

MOST PLAY SETS BEGIN AS KITS OF SOME TYPE THAT MUST BE ASSEMBLED. The set depicted on these pages includes a number of common features—an elevated fort, a ladder, and a swing beam. (A similar structure, with how-to photos and building tips, is highlighted on pages 98 to 103.) This type of set can be put together by one person with basic tools, but a helper or two will make the project go much more quickly and smoothly. The following step-by-step instructions will help you get a sense of what building a play set actually entails so you can decide whether to do it yourself or hire a pro.

A combination play set like this one can be built near trees to create a tree house effect.

1 **ASSEMBLE THE DECK FRAME.** With a rubber mallet, pound a bolt with washer through a predrilled hole. Leave the nut only hand-tightened so you can adjust the structure to be plumb and square until it is erect.

2 **SECURE BOARDS TO BEAMS.** The bottom brace uses lag bolts. Holes for lag bolts and wood screws are generally not predrilled on these types of structures, and there are several of them. Since you'll probably be using a socket wrench, you'll need to predrill every hole and then tighten all the bolts with a wrench.

3 **ERECT THE POSTS.** To do this without a helper, wrap your leg around a post to hold it upright while attaching a bottom brace. When both post assemblies are up, push handfuls of mulch under low spots until the structure is level.

4 **ASSEMBLE THE FLOORING SECTIONS.** If they come preassembled in a kit, you will only need to bolt them in place. Tighten the nuts after checking to make sure the diagonal distance between opposite corners is equal, a sign that the floor is square, not trapezoidal.

5 **ERECT THE FORT.** With the floor in place, use it as a platform to erect the rest of the fort. Add the remaining beams, then the rails, which also typically come preassembled.

6 **ATTACH THE ROOF.** Assembling a tarp roof is a snap—literally. Screws with snap heads hold it in place. With the screws snapped on, drape the fabric in place and tap with a hammer to mark their locations. Then unsnap the screws and fasten them to the wood.

7 **ATTACH THE LADDER WITH LAG BOLTS.** If the gap between the top rung of the ladder and the fort's deck exceeds 3½ inches, block it with a board so that kids don't get stuck in it.

8 **ATTACH THE SLIDE.** If the slide comes in one piece, this should be quick because it takes just two pan head screws, which are wide and flat on the back. If burrs or rough areas develop, set the screw head deeper, sand the hold edge, and add a dab of silicone caulk to fix them.

9 **BUILD THE SWING BEAM.** Before you construct the beam, install the swing hangers while the beam is still on the ground. With a special A-frame brace loosely bolted to the posts and the swing beam, rest one beam end on the fort and hoist the other end until the posts swing underneath and give support. Check to make sure the beam is level before final tightening.

GET IN THE SWING

SWINGS HAVE COME A LONG WAY SINCE THE DAYS OF THE TARZAN-STYLE KNOTTED ROPE dangling from a tree, although the appeal of these old-fashioned swings remains. To suit multiple kids, either hang different types of swings in one large structure or substitute more-challenging swings as kids grow.

Select swings with these age and developmental levels in mind:

- **BIRTH TO 2 YEARS.** Full-bucket swing seats provide support on all sides and prevent the youngest swingers from falling out. A high-back infant swing with a seat belt is another option.
- **2 TO 5 YEARS.** Before age 3, full-bucket seats are still the safest bet. Half-bucket seats, with protective chains across the open area, are suitable for preschoolers. Gliders allow one or two kids to ride gently as their motor skills develop. Kindergarten-age children can enjoy twirling with friends in a tire swing or learn how to propel themselves on standard belt swings.
- **5 TO 12 YEARS.** Once they've tired of traditional swings, older kids can indulge in disc, buoy ball, and trapeze swings.

How to Install It

Whether you are building a new structure or adding to an existing one, installing a swing requires few materials and steps. With the exception of tire swings, most swings are composed of the following:

- Two swing hangers including eyebolts or T bolts, washers, and nuts
- Two spring-loaded clips
- S hooks (in some kits)
- Chain or rope
- Two chain-to-seat connectors (varies depending on swing type)
- One swing seat

Hammocks

A laid-back cousin of the swing, a hammock is perfect for rocking and relaxing. Hammocks come in many different styles and range in materials from cotton rope to nylon netting. Synthetic hammocks are more durable than those made of natural materials, but they are sometimes less comfortable, so be sure to try before you buy. Most hammocks are sold with stands since so few backyards have the required perfectly spaced pair of trees.

To suspend the swing, choose either metal chains or synthetic fiber ropes. Metal chains are the sturdiest option; they should be galvanized to prevent rust. Or opt for colorful plastic-coated chains so small fingers don't get pinched. Nylon or Dacron ropes are other options that won't rot. (Natural-fiber ropes such as hemp can rot or fray.)

To attach a swing to a beam, use only the hardware designed for it and follow the manufacturer's instructions. Generally, you'll drill a hole through the center of the beam, then insert an eyebolt or T bolt through the hole, securing it on top with a washer and two nuts. Attach a spring-loaded clip to the eyebolt, then either attach the chain directly to that, or attach an S hook before the chain if it doesn't fit through the clip. Because open S hooks can catch clothing, pinch them closed with pliers or a hammer. Gaps in S hooks should be no greater than 0.04 inches (about 1 millimeter); to test, you should not be able to fit a dime into the space.

For standard swings, the two hangers above an individual swing should be an adequate distance apart; experts recommend at least 20 inches but the distance may vary depending on the product you buy. Swing seats should also be spaced an adequate distance from structure posts (approximately 30 inches) and adjacent seats (24 inches).

For preschoolers, hang swings from pivots located no more than 8 feet above the landing surface; seats for this age group should be no less than 12 inches above the ground. Seats for school-age children (5 and older) should hang no less than 16 inches above ground. For maximum safety, experts recommend hanging full-bucket tot swings in separate structures or in separate bays of the same structure.

Swings seats made of lightweight rubber or plastic are generally preferable to heavier metal or wood seats, which can cause greater injury if a child is struck by them. Look for bucket and belt seats made of soft rubber, canvas, plastic, or hard but lightweight polyethylene. Trapeze bars are typically constructed of zinc-plated steel and may have a plastic coating. Whatever material you choose, make sure seat edges are smoothly finished or rounded.

A GALLERY OF SWINGS

AT THE END OF THE DAY, A SWING is probably the most classic, enduring plaything you can install in your backyard. Swings can fit in yards of any size and style. Even adults can't resist the joy of sailing through the air on one of the many types of swings that can be hung from tree branches, play sets, or their own frames.

ABOVE: With a tall, sturdy tree, all you need to construct a great swing is thick rope running through a piece of wood, plus eyebolts, washers, and clips. FAR LEFT: A disc swing can be built with simple materials like wood and rope. LEFT: For older kids and adults who seek more peaceful modes of suspension, hammock swings are a relaxing option.

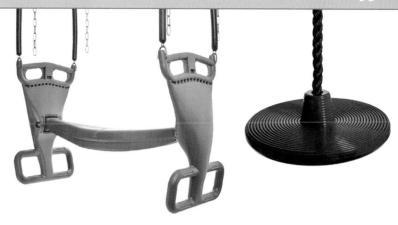

LEFT: **A bouncy swing lets kids experience an up-and-down motion in addition to the usual back and forth.** ABOVE: **Gliders accommodate one or two swingers, who can use the openings at the ends to place their hands and feet.** ABOVE RIGHT: **Plastic disc swings often come with play sets, but they can also be purchased as add-ons.**

These twin swings are hung from a beam covered by a rich patina of plants and flowers, which hides the hardware connecting the ropes to the beam and makes them blend seamlessly into the garden landscape. The blue color of the seats also complements the surrounding plants. Underneath is a thick layer of wood chips for gentle landings.

BACKYARD CLASSIC

LONG BEFORE SWING SETS WERE INVENTED, tire swings were staples in many backyards. They still are. The most familiar style, the tire hung by rope from a tree, is also the simplest to engineer. All you need is a tall, sturdy tree, some rope, and a tire.

The tree should be strong enough to support the weight of the tire and the heaviest child who will use the swing. Hardwood trees like oak, walnut, sugar maple, ash, cherry, or beech are best. Trees to avoid include fast-growing, soft-limbed varieties like silver maple, box elder, willow, or poplar. Ideally the branch should be a minimum 8 to 10 feet from the ground and horizontal. Make sure it also measures 6 to 8 inches in diameter where you attach the swing. Use common sense in making sure that the rope is not hung too close to the tree's trunk or any surrounding objects, and also not too close to the ground so your child can swing freely and safely.

Use a spare tire or pick one up at a tire store or junkyard. Avoid steel-belted tires, whose sharp cords might eventually work their way out of the rubber sheathing. Clean the tire thoroughly and coat it with vinyl or rubber sealant to protect it from the elements and prevent clothing stains. Drill a few holes in the part of the tire that will hang nearest the ground to allow rainwater to drain. Or buy a lightweight plastic tire designed for kids' play.

An old-fashioned tire swing is an irresistible lure for kids. Note how the one above is a safe distance from a strong, sturdy tree, and that the rope is wrapped around the tire several times.

For hanging, purchase rope made of nylon or Dacron (a polyester fiber), which are more durable materials than hemp or polypropylene. Like the tree, the rope must be strong enough to support the weight of both the tire and the child. When purchasing rope, ask about its tensile strength, which should be equal to, at minimum, the weight of the tire and heaviest user. Most climbing ropes have a tensile strength measured in the thousands of pounds, which should be more than sufficient. You'll need enough rope for the height of the swing plus an additional 10 feet for loops and knots. To protect the tree and the rope from wear and tear, slip a piece of rubber over the portion of rope that wraps around the limb.

Wrap one end of the rope around the branch a few times and secure it with a single or double bowline knot (see illustrations at right). Finish with a stopper knot, which prevents slippage. Repeat the steps to attach the rope to the tire at the other end.

You can also hang the swing as you would attach a swing seat to a play structure—with an eyebolt, washers and nuts, links, and a chain. If you go this route, you'll need to drill a hole all the way through the center of the branch to insert the eyebolt. Secure it with a washer and nuts on both sides of the bolt, then do the same with the tire. Use quick links to attach the chain to each eyebolt.

With either assembly method, spread mulch around the tree to protect the roots and provide padding for falls. Then test the swing yourself, making any adjustments before kids use it.

Double bowline: Make two loops in the rope and wind the end of the rope around the tire twice; then thread the rope up through the loops, around the rope above the loops, and back down through the loops again.

Basic bowline (top): Make a loop in the rope and wind the end of the rope around the tire twice; then thread the rope up through the loop, around the rope above the loop, and back down through the loop again. For extra security against slippage, finish with a stopper knot (above).

Tire Swings for Play Structures

Many swing set manufacturers offer ready-made tire swings with coated chains as accessories. You can find one that swings from two chains on a single axis or from three chains in all directions. Keep in mind that the tire should hang from its own structure, or from a separate bay in a structure, to create a safety zone. At its highest swinging point, the tire should be at least 30 inches away from structure posts.

GETTING UP AND DOWN

FROM AN EARLY AGE, KIDS HAVE A NATURAL URGE TO CLIMB UP, come down, and climb back up again. This need can be fulfilled by just taking a look around your yard and seeing what you have to work with, such as trees, hills, walls, or decks. Through creative use of your environment, you can incorporate ladders, climbing walls, and slides without installing a full play set.

For kids, learning how to scale a rope with knots along its length, or a rope ladder hung from a tree, is its own reward. These features are inexpensive and easy to set up in almost any yard with a strong tree that has thick branches. Materials are available at most hardware stores.

Build it and they will climb! Use plastic rocks to create a climbing wall on the side of your house or other sturdy structure. It saves space and provides a fun form of exercise.

Don't let a slope in your yard prevent your kids from enjoying climbing adventures. A climbing feature or slide can be installed on or next to a playhouse built at the top of a hill (above left). Or stairs can be installed next to a slide (above right).

RIGHT: There are three ways to reach this deck: A regular set of stairs, a climbing wall, and a rope hung from a rail that dangles over the climbing wall. FAR RIGHT: To get to this tree house, kids have to scale a fairly steep ladder whose rungs double as handholds.

BUILDING A PLAY SET

CLIMB, SWING, SLIDE, AND SCOOP SAND ON THIS COMBINATION PLAY STRUCTURE. BUILT FROM A KIT BY FRIENDS, THIS SET OFFERS FUN FOR KIDS AGES 10 AND UNDER

David and Violette Sofaer of San Jose, California, wanted to give their young kids, Zeke and Miranda, a play set they could grow up with, but they had a limited amount of open space in their backyard. Measuring just 14 by 13 feet, this precut play-set kit from Swing-N-Slide was a good solution for their family. With an elevated, shaded platform at its heart and accessories on every side, the play set packs in plenty of adventure and activities.

Before the Sofaers and their crew began to build, they needed to decide where to position the structure so that it could be seen from the house, but not so close that their barbecue and outdoor dining area would feel overrun with kids. Their modest backyard didn't give them many choices, but after carefully considering the rectangular orientation of their lawn, they chose to install the slide on the left side of the play set (rather than on its right side as shown in the plans) so that the structure could be positioned as close as possible to the back fence—and, just as important, so that kids using the slide would have the greatest amount of safe landing space. Though not described in the plans, this simple customization was easy to accomplish.

Kits like this one typically include all hardware and precut pieces of wood except the main 4 × 4s, which you can pick up at your local lumberyard. While this kit is meant to be constructed in a single day, don't be surprised if it takes you a weekend or longer.

Four kids at a time can safely play on this structure. Its compact footprint offers multiple challenges and activities, yet fits comfortably in a modest backyard.

TOP LEFT: One of three climbing features leading to the platform (four if you count the slide!), this molded plastic climbing wall has several footholds to make it easy for Bryan to scramble onto the deck.

TOP RIGHT: The floor of the platform and the accessories leading to it create a shady spot for sand play. Although shallow, the sandbox works just fine for preschooler Sydney.

BOTTOM LEFT: What kid doesn't enjoy a ride down a slide? This one that Clayton is about to try comes in two pieces that are bolted together. The horizontal cross piece at the top of the slide discourages use by larger kids and adults, for whom the slide is not explictly designed.

BOTTOM RIGHT: Aye, aye, matey! With her bright yellow wheel in hand, Sara can pretend she's a captain steering clear of danger.

Tools List

WHAT THEY SAY YOU NEED

- Electric drill and Phillips bit
- Socket wrench set
- Hammer
- Tape measure
- Safety glasses and dust mask
- Carpenter's square

WHAT HELPS GET THE JOB DONE

- Rubber mallet
- Cordless drill with extra battery pack
- Work gloves
- Pliers
- Level

Main Structure

1 **ATTACH INTERLOCKING BRACKETS TO 4 × 4 POSTS.** Measure the spacing of the brackets carefully and examine them closely to determine that you're using the right ones and clipping them together correctly. Check that the holes line up before securing the brackets with 2-inch lag screws. Angle the screws slightly toward the center of the posts so you don't inadvertently drive them through the outside edge.

2 **ASSEMBLE THE FRAMES.** The vertical posts and horizontal boards create two frames that form the skeleton of the play set when connected to each other. To set up this connection, measure and attach the lower and upper boards to the posts. Use a square to ensure that the boards are at right angles to the posts.

3 **CONNECT FRAMES WITH 4 × 4 BEAMS.** Use the kit-supplied 4 × 4s to connect the frames to each other and create the edges of the platform's floor. Have a helper push from the opposite side of the structure to stabilize it as you install the lag screws through the bracket holes. The frame will get heavier as you build, so determine if the structure is exactly where you want it before installing the floor.

Inventory Alert!

Before you build, take inventory to make sure you have all supplied materials plus the lumber you needed to purchase on your own. Organize the wood and hardware so everything is easy to locate. Early on, the builders of this kit discovered they were missing hardware. A call to the company's customer-service line, followed by a trip to the lumberyard, allowed most of the construction to continue; other fasteners had to be shipped and installed later.

Floor and Rails

1 **INSTALL THE CENTER FLOOR JOIST.** As you construct the platform floor, as well as other sections of the kit, don't be afraid to improvise with tools the manufacturer's official tool list may not include. We used a mallet, shown here, to tap the center floor joist into position.

2 **ATTACH THE SHORT FLOOR BOARDS.** Place the two short floor boards at either end of the floor area; measure to make sure they are parallel. Tap the boards into place between the posts and secure them with screws, including one through the center floor joist.

3 **SECURE THE REMAINING FLOOR BOARDS.** Inspect both sides of each board to choose the side you want facing up. Lay out the boards and space them as evenly as possible by the eyeball method, or use a pencil or other small tool to create more precise gaps. Attach the boards to the framing with two screws at either end and two along the center joist.

4 **INSTALL THE HORIZONTAL RAIL BOARDS.** Now that the deck floor is constructed, you can stand on it to build the rest of the structure. Some of the horizontal boards will secure the vertical pickets that will prevent kids from leaving the platform on the swing side; others will guide kids to the safest access points for the slide and climbing features.

Swings

1 **MEASURE FOR THE SWINGS.** With a tape measure, mark the holes where the swing hangers will attach. It's easier to do this on the ground before the structure is erected and the swing beam is over your head. Use a $3/8$-inch bit to drill holes; tap in the T nuts with a hammer.

2 **USE THE BRACKET TO CREATE AN A-FRAME.** Lay out the 4 × 4 beams and align their edges with the edges of the frame bracket, with the bracket facing outward as shown. Before securing the bracket completely with screws, lay out the 2 × 4 cross member to make sure it is positioned as shown in the instructions across the 4 × 4s. Flip the frame over to install the second bracket.

3 **ATTACH THE A-FRAME TO THE SWING BEAM.** Using a mallet, tap the hex bolt in gradually before ratcheting securely. Make sure the tightened bolt is flush or near flush with the top of the T nut. Repeat with the second bracket and bolt hole. The first bracket hole may line up more easily with the bolt hole than the second one.

4 **SECURE THE SWING BEAM TO THE STRUCTURE.** Lift the A-frame, tipping it upright so that the end of the swing beam lines up with the bracket installed on the beam above the platform. Double-check that it's level, then secure it with screws.

Finishing Touches

1 **ATTACH THE "ROCKS" TO THE CLIMBING WALL.** After constructing the wall on the ground, place the plastic rocks in positions that will create a climbing route for kids. Choose the route carefully, then drill holes for bolts and T nuts. Make sure none of the rocks are positioned too close to the edges of the wall.

2 **SECURE THE WALL TO THE FRAME.** The instructions called for drilling screws through the small corner of 2 × 4 (the part that is under the platform) and then into each 4 × 4, but the builders decided that a ³⁄₈-inch bolt with a T nut on the inside and a recessed head on the outside would be stronger.

The periscope can be installed anywhere on the play set. In this case, it was attached to the side of the structure that offered the best view of the house.

In addition to locations for two standard swings (choose a bucket for toddlers or a regular strap seat for older kids), this play set also features room for a disc swing.

CABLE RIDE

WHOOSH! ADD THIS EXHILARATING ACTIVITY TO YOUR YARD AND IT CAN BE THE HIT OF THE NEIGHBORHOOD

If you've never been on a cable ride, chances are you'll grin ear to ear the first time you take one. Riders grip a trolley device, lift up their feet, and zip down a length of steel cable before coming to a gentle stop as the cable ascends near its end.

While not every space can accommodate a cable ride, the best situation is a level or slightly sloping yard with two sturdy trees at least 40 feet apart to use as end posts. If anchor trees don't exist, it's possible to build artificial supports, but this requires thick, well-braced posts set 4 to 5 feet deep into concrete. Do not attach cables to masonry walls, roof overhangs, or other structures without much strength. The cable route must be clear of obstructions for 6 feet on either side and should be located away from paths or other places where people walk. Metal cable presents a real hazard if passersby hit it with their head or throat.

Plastic trolleys suitable for children's rides up to 70 feet are sold as kits, and heavier-duty metal trolleys, which can go for 150 feet or more, are sold as parts for systems you assemble yourself (see Resources). The kits include instructions for installing the cable so that it has the right amount of slack to provide a fun ride and a safe stopping point. Check the kit's weight limit—some max out at 100 pounds, while others can accommodate adults.

Materials List

- Trolley
- Stainless-steel (type 304) aircraft-grade cable: $1/4$" for rides under 150'; $3/8$" for longer runs
- Lawn tractor replacement tire
- Galvanized eye-jaw turnbuckle, $3/4$" × 18"
- Stainless-steel thimble
- Nine stainless-steel cable clamps

FOR PREFERRED ATTACHMENT SYSTEM

- Two forged $5/8$" eyebolts, long enough to go through anchor trees at attachment height with 2" to spare
- Two nuts, two lock washers, and two flat washers to fit bolts

FOR ALTERNATE ATTACHMENT SYSTEM

- Old bicycle tire
- Enough extra cable to loop around trees

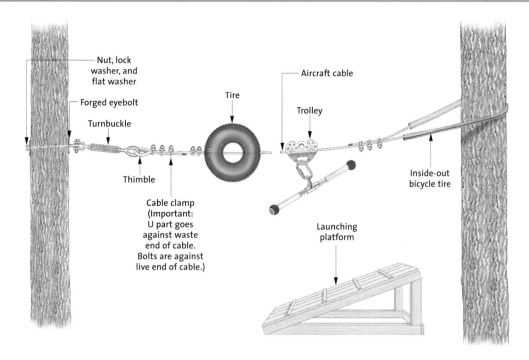

Nut, lock washer, and flat washer

Forged eyebolt

Turnbuckle

Aircraft cable

Tire

Trolley

Thimble

Cable clamp (Important: U part goes against waste end of cable. Bolts are against live end of cable.)

Inside-out bicycle tire

Launching platform

**PREFERRED ATTACHMENT
SYSTEM FOR EACH END**

**ALTERNATE ATTACHMENT
SYSTEM FOR EACH END**

The metal cable on which the trolley rides must be attached so that it is slightly higher at the beginning point than at the end, or the rider will stall in the middle. Some experts recommend a rise of 6 inches per 10 feet and a starting point 2½ feet taller than the tallest rider; others say to start 15 feet off the ground and end at 5 feet, so there's a good deal of variability in what you can do in your backyard. The amount of slack also makes a difference. Test the setup to make sure that the tallest riders won't hit their feet on the ground at the lowest point of the ride.

Although kits call for slack and gravity to stop riders at the end, it's a good idea to install a tire bumper. Attach the cable to forged eyebolts inserted through the trees, rather than wrapping the cable around the trunks, as some kits specify. Be sure to buy forged eyebolts as standard eyescrews can pull out, snap, or open.

Cable looped around trees can wear through bark and injure the critical cambium layer below. If you do decide to attach the cable this way, rest the cable in a sling, such as an inside-out bicycle tire. Avoid wrapping cable tightly against a tree because it will force the cable into a sharp bend, which will weaken it. Align cable clamps so the round section lies against the main stretch of the cable. The screw section goes against the short end of the cable.

Cable rides require regular inspection. After every 50 rides or so, check the bolts and tighten them if necessary. Replace any cable that has frayed.

CONNECTION AT FAR END
Start with the turnbuckle extended as far open as possible. Grip the cable with pliers and pull until it is as tight as you can make it. Lightly fasten the cable clamps and check tension. You may need to repeat this several times until the cable is taut enough. Then tighten the cable clamps, taking care not to overtighten. Make the final adjustment with the turnbuckle. Check all connections frequently and retighten as needed.

sports
&
games

A BACKYARD CAN HOST A WIDE RANGE OF ATHLETIC
ACTIVITIES WHILE PROVIDING KIDS WITH A PRIVATE PLACE
TO PRACTICE THEIR SKILLS. THIS CHAPTER DETAILS HOW
TO CONSTRUCT CHALLENGING PROPS FOR BIKES AND
SKATEBOARDS, AND OFFERS DIMENSIONS FOR BASKETBALL
COURTS, BASEBALL DIAMONDS, AND SOCCER FIELDS.

BACKYARDS FOR PLAY

WITH SOME CREATIVE PLANNING, YOU CAN PRO-VIDE KIDS WITH OPPORTUNITIES to perfect their baseball pitch, shoot hoops, or reach new heights on a trampoline. In many cases, you can pur-chase kits or gear that make staging a sport in the backyard effortless and economical. Or you can build equipment like a skateboard ramp from scratch. The degree of realism you bring to the endeavor—replicating the dimension of a regulation soccer field, building a pitcher's mound—is up to you.

To create an athletic backyard environment for young kids, you may need nothing more than a scaled-down basketball hoop, T-ball set, or trampoline. Beginners' sports equipment, which is usually plastic and lightweight, is easy to come by, store, and pass on to relatives or neighbors when kids out-grow it. As kids' interests develop, consider buying or building more chal-lenging, realistic equipment that can help them sharpen their skills. Fields and ball courts, with regulation dimensions and accessories, may take up space, but they can provide years of exciting activity.

In the privacy of their backyard, kids often bend the rules by jump-ing two at a time on a tramp.

Versatility is also key, especially since a child's interests can quickly shift. Talk to kids about their pas-sions and aim for a yard that fills multiple needs. On a flat stretch of lawn, you can play mini golf one day and badminton the next. A concrete or asphalt basketball half-court could also accommodate a net for volley-ball. To make it convenient to go from one activity to another—and to preserve space for non-sport activi-ties—consider equipment that's easy to move and store, like a roller hockey goal or a skateboard rail. Also, in addition to organized sports, don't forget classic games like tag or cap-ture the flag, which don't require much more than energy and a will-ingness to goof off.

Before your child joins his first official T-ball team, he can get some practice time in with the help of a ball, a bat, and an actual home plate. Similarly, a basketball hoop allows him to try-try again, and perhaps learn a few tricks from you, so that when it's game time, he'll be ready.

The Benefits of Fun and Games

Even tag, the most basic of children's games, provides a good physical workout. Many others that require minimal or no equipment at all teach the payoff of practice, focus, and fairness.

GAME	BENEFIT
Badminton	Agility, eye-hand coordination, flexibility, speed, team play
Baseball	Eye-hand coordination, speed, strength, team play
Basketball	Agility, endurance, speed, strength, team play
Capture the flag	Speed, stamina, team play
Cycling	Balance, endurance, flexibility, stamina, strength
Dodgeball	Agility, flexibility, speed, team play
Frisbee	Eye-hand coordination, flexibility, speed
Hacky sack	Agility, balance, eye-foot coordination
Jump rope	Endurance, stamina
Skateboarding	Balance, coordination, core strength
Soccer	Agility, endurance, speed, stamina, strength, team play
Tag	Endurance, speed, stamina
Trampoline	Agility, balance, coordination

A GALLERY OF PLAYFUL SPACES

DESIGNATING PARTS OF YOUR BACK-YARD FOR SPORTS, games, and other activities need not crowd out adult areas or detract from the beauty of your landscape. With some planning and creative design, you can meet everyone's needs. Grass, shrubs, and flowers can easily coexist with almost any fun your children can dream up. In fact, the more garden you have in your backyard, the better. Backyards with well-tended and diverse gardens send a message to kids that this is a space they must share with you. And if you find it too tough to teach your children not to trample your precious perennials, don't be ashamed to play it safe by placing the hardiest and toughest plants near their play areas.

BELOW: **Young kids and adults alike love trains. This outdoor railroad track winds through a miniature forest of special dwarf varieties of shrubs that are roughly the same scale as the train.**

Croquet, anyone? This classic lawn game is easy to set up and put away, and it can be played by just about every member of the family, regardless of their athletic ability.

Do Fence Me In

To contain all the action in your yard—and away from neighbors and the street—consider a barrier or fencing. In addition to wood and chain-link fences, there's almost invisible netting, typically made of nylon mesh or polyethylene, with small square or diamond holes that keep balls from escaping but allow sunlight in. It comes in a range of dimensions, and you can make it retractable or fix it to existing fences or to steel posts.

NORTH SHORE CYCLING

KIDS TAKE THEIR BIKING SKILLS TO A NEW LEVEL WITH TEETER-TOTTERS, MINI ROLLER COASTERS, AND OTHER OBSTACLES THEY BUILD THEMSELVES

In mountain biking circles, the "North Shore" style of freeriding is considered one of the most exciting. Freeriding on its own combines the obstacle-course concept of "trials" biking with the jumping and speed incorporated in BMX racing. North Shore devotees take it further by riding their bikes on trails laced with obstacles, such as teeter-totters, narrow log bridges, and multi-tiered jumps. In the extreme, it's a sport most parents would prefer their kids admire only from a distance. Toned down, however, it's great backyard fun.

Christian, 15, was hooked after a family visit to a resort that offered freerider trails suitable for cyclists of all skill levels. Back home, Christian set about building routes of his own, mostly with scrap wood. Because rigging up new challenges is half the fun, he doesn't worry about building contraptions that will withstand the elements or last a long time. He builds, masters the trick, and then starts inventing fresh feats to test his skill.

Two years ago, a track flat on the ground seemed challenging. Now, that's something he builds to introduce younger kids, including 8-year-old Sam, to the sport.

Building a Teeter-Totter

A teeter-totter for bicycle riders consists of a base topped by a slatted frame that pivots on a $\frac{1}{2}$-inch galvanized bolt threaded through holes in the frame.

The teeter-totter must be designed so that it returns to the starting position on its own. There are two easy options for making this happen: Either make the front section (where the biker enters) a few inches longer than the exit, the solution used here, or add a weight underneath the entry area.

Materials List

- Two supports and uprights, 2 × 4 × 12'
- Two base pieces, 2 × 6 × 10'
- Cross pieces, cut from three 1 × 4 × 10' boards
- One galvanized bolt, $\frac{1}{2}$" × 12", with two $\frac{1}{2}$" flat washers and one nut
- Galvanized deck screws or nails, $1\frac{5}{8}$" and $2\frac{1}{2}$"

FOR EACH ADDITIONAL TRACK SECTION

- Two base pieces, 2 × 4 × 12'
- Cross pieces cut from three 1 × 4 × 10' boards
- Galvanized deck screws or nails, $1\frac{5}{8}$"

Although a teeter-totter can serve as a stand-alone place to practice, connecting it to other sections of track makes riding more fun. Christian makes all sections the same width and just butts them together when they are on the ground. When he elevates tracks, he screws sections together and to their supports.

ABOVE: Having mastered the basics of freeriding, Christian adds new challenges by creating tracks that are higher and skinnier. To make sure the tracks won't slip off his sawhorses, he screws the support pieces to wide boards and then screws those boards to the sawhorses. For an elevated teeter-totter, he adds a diagonal brace at the pivot point and attaches a 1 × 2 vertical guide to the top to make sure the track doesn't slip sideways, off the base.

LEFT: To allow the teeter-totter to pivot easily, avoid over-tightening the nut on the bolt.

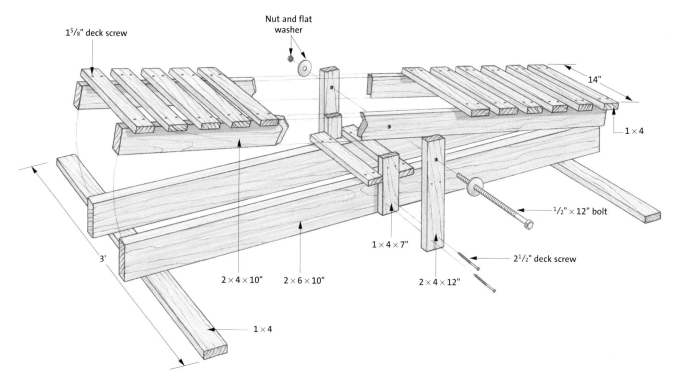

$1^5/8$" deck screw

Nut and flat washer

14"

1 × 4

3'

$^1/2$" × 12" bolt

1 × 4 × 7"

2 × 4 × 10"   2 × 6 × 10"

2½" deck screw

2 × 4 × 12"

1 × 4

Building a Roller Coaster

An easy North Shore–style roller coaster is made up of a series of wooden humps topped by wooden slats. For a beginners' course, Christian made the humps about 8 inches higher than the base track and cut the support pieces into a curve about 4 feet wide. He drew the shape freehand and cut it with a reciprocating saw, although a jigsaw or coping saw will also work.

Christian spaced the humps so that the peaks were about 8 feet apart. Sam, trying the ride for the first time (left), got over the first hump easily, then veered off onto the lawn. With a ride so low to the ground, he had no difficulty remaining upright to the end.

Materials List

- Base pieces: two 2 × 8 × 12', two 2 × 8 × 8'
- Cross pieces cut from four 1 × 4 × 8' boards
- Galvanized deck screws or nails, 1⅝"

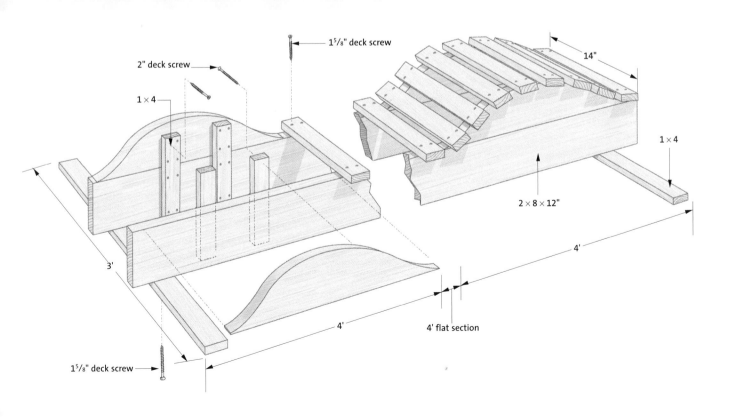

Building a Jump Ramp

A jump ramp allows a biker to experience the momentary thrill of becoming airborne. Although he's built ramps of wood, Christian says dirt ramps are easier to build and adjust. A little difference in the curve, especially near the lip, affects how high the rider can get.

To avoid having to shovel too much dirt, he stacks firewood as a base. (Hay bales or rocks will also work.) Two big pieces of firewood placed vertically in the middle give good support for the top of the jump. Smaller pieces go horizontally, perpendicular to the direction the rider will travel. Wedge-shaped pieces of plywood screwed to the firewood create the rough shape for the launching-ramp sides. Christian fills in the remaining space with dirt (right). Packing it in tight, he shapes the top of the pile into a curved lip.

On the back half of the woodpile, Christian lays down a piece of ½-inch plywood as a landing ramp. This ramp is very important because it eases the effect of the landing on the rider's spine. Christian's found that plywood stands up to the force of impact better than dirt. He makes the landing ramp a little lower and a little less steep than the launching ramp.

For beginners, Christian fills in the space between the launching ramp and the landing ramp. As riders become more experienced, they usually want a real gap (and higher ramps).

Materials List

- Assorted firewood pieces
- Plywood, ½" (or thicker), one piece approximately 2' × 4', one approximately 2' × 2'
- Two plywood wedges, about 3' long, angled from 6" to 12" wide (or more)
- About a dozen nails or screws
- Dirt

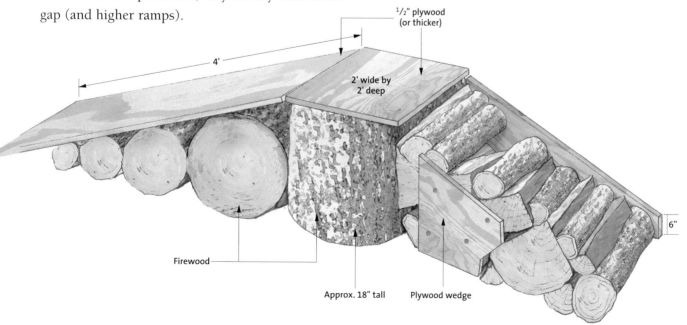

½" plywood (or thicker)

4'

2' wide by 2' deep

Firewood

Approx. 18" tall

Plywood wedge

6"

STREET SMARTS

BRING THE EXTREME SPORT SPIRIT HOME WITH A SKATEBOARDING RAMP OR RAIL. BUILD IT YOURSELF, OR CHOOSE FROM THE NUMEROUS PRODUCTS DESIGNED FOR BOARD PLAY

Built with the help of a carpenter, this skate ramp is big enough for Mitch to practice tricks on it with a board or skates, and lightweight enough so Mitch's parents can shove it out of the way.

For kids who love to test their physical limits, a backyard ramp takes skateboarding to a whole different level. You can build a ramp with basic materials such as plywood and screws, or you can buy one ready-made. Grinding rails, benches, and other products also offer challenging surfaces for hours of practice and play.

What to Look For

Go to a skate shop or a sporting goods store, or search online to check out different types of skating or boarding surfaces and decide which is best. Your budding skateboarder may want to start with a low-level grinding rail or bench. A skilled skater will enjoy a wedge or launch ramp. In a spacious driveway, you can even create an obstacle course with multiple pieces or combination structures.

Building a Ramp

If you decide to build your own ramp, the trickiest part of the construction is the first step: establishing a curve that will allow the skater to become airborne. To simplify the process, use a 1 × 2 about 8 feet long as a compass. Extend a 3-inch screw through the piece 2 inches from one end to create a pivot point; 88 inches past that, drill a hole wide enough for a pencil. Working on a flat lawn or other suitable surface, poke the pivot screw into the ground at the distances shown in the illustration on the opposite page.

Depending on the setup, you may need to have one person apply slight pressure while another person moves the compass in an arc to trace the curved line on one of the side pieces. Cut out the curved piece with a jigsaw. Trace the shape to make two more pieces the same size. Next, prepare the framing pieces.

Materials List

- Eight 2 × 4 × 8' framing pieces
- One sheet ³⁄₄" exterior plywood
- Two sheets ¹⁄₄" exterior plywood (marine grade preferred)
- Eighteen ³⁄₈" × 5" lag screws, with washers
- Galvanized or coated screws, 2" and 3"
- Heavy-duty 1" galvanized staples
- Thin piece of wood, about 1 × 2 × 8', to use as compass

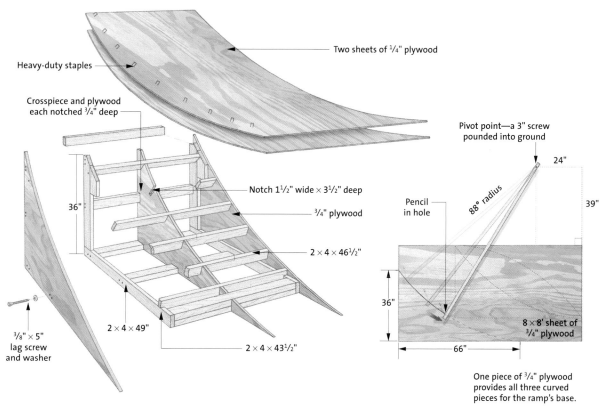

Two sheets of ¼" plywood

Heavy-duty staples

Crosspiece and plywood
each notched ¾" deep

Notch 1½" wide × 3½" deep

¾" plywood

2 × 4 × 46½"

2 × 4 × 49"

2 × 4 × 43½"

36"

⅜" × 5"
lag screw
and washer

Pivot point—a 3" screw
pounded into ground

24"

88° radius

39"

Pencil
in hole

36"

66"

8 × 8' sheet of
¾" plywood

One piece of ¾" plywood
provides all three curved
pieces for the ramp's base.

Cut the wood to make seven pieces 43½ inches long, five 46½ inches long, two 49 inches long, and two 36 inches long. Save the two longest scraps.

Using one of the curved plywood pieces as a template, trace the top part of the curve onto one end of each 36-inch piece and each scrap piece—with a jigsaw. Then screw together the back and bottom of the frame as shown using 3-inch screws. You will need to cut a notch across one of the wide faces of the crosspiece that goes at the center back—the notch in the support will slip into it.

Select two of the curved plywood pieces for the sides and attach them to the other framing pieces with lag screws, as shown. Use the remaining plywood piece for the ramp's center support. In the center piece, cut a notch 3½ inches wide and ¾ inch deep at the center of the back edge. Also notch the plywood so it will fit around the crosspieces at the rear of the ramp.

On the curved edge of this piece of plywood, cut six notches 3½ inches deep and 1½ inches wide. Locate them so that the first notch is 14 inches from the top corner and the others are approximately 7 inches apart. After you cut these notches, use the plywood as a template to mark the locations on the side plywood pieces.

Screw the center plywood support to the framing with 2-inch screws. Slip in the 2 × 4s that will support the top of the ramp and attach them with 2-inch screws. Staple on the ¼-inch plywood, one sheet at a time, leaving the excess in the front. If necessary, add a few screws to lock the plywood in place. Sink the screw heads just enough so they are flush with the surface.

This skatepark-style ramp by SunRamp is made for home use.

Practice on a grind rail, with adjustable height, from MojoRail.

NOTHING BUT NETS

BRING FAST-PACED NBA ACTION TO YOUR YARD WITH A BASKETBALL HOOP. For pickup games or free-throw practice, you can purchase a portable hoop with adjustable basket height or install a more permanent one. Adjustable hoops make more sense for families with young kids, but mounted hoops take up less space, so they may work better in small yards and driveways. Serious hoop dreamers can paint or draw a set of court dimensions (called a key) on the ground to stage half-court competitions.

Backboard Installation

First, select a level, smooth, and unobstructed playing surface. The driveway or a patio may fit the bill. Next, visit a sporting goods or home improvement store or go online to buy a basketball goal kit that includes the rim, net, and backboard. You may have to purchase mounting brackets separately; choose brackets designed for your mounting structure—a roof or solid wall.

A regulation-size half court measures 47 feet long by 50 feet wide. The backboard should be installed in the middle of the baseline. Position the rim 10 feet above the playing surface. The distance between the baseline and the free throw line is 19 feet.

Backboards are typically made of wood, fiberglass, or acrylic. Acrylic is a durable material for outdoors and provides a good surface for rebounding. If you choose fiberglass, make sure it's $1/2$-inch thick for adequate rebounding. Regulation dimensions for a backboard are 72 by 42 inches, but you may want a slightly smaller one depending on the size of your playing area. Also look for a "break-away" rim designed to bend a bit for dunking. You'll need a ladder, drill, and level, as well as a helper since kit pieces are heavy.

Wall-mounted. If the wall you choose is just below a flat roof (for example, you're mounting the hoop on a garage door), assemble the support brackets and place them on the wall a couple of inches below the roof's soffit. The front edge of each bracket should extend past the rain gutter; use wood spacers under the bracket if necessary. (Otherwise, position the bracket so the rim will be at regulation height, or 10 feet above the playing surface.) Make sure the bracket is level, and secure it to wall studs with long lag screws. Attach the backboard to the brackets with carriage bolts and install the hoop.

Roof-mounted. For a slanted roof, assemble brackets according to the manufacturer's instructions. Place the brackets on the roof so their front edges clear the rain gutter; use wood spacers to raise brackets if necessary. Fasten the brackets with lag screws through the roofing and sheathing and into the rafters. Seal the holes with roofing cement. Attach the backboard to the brackets with carriage bolts and install the hoop.

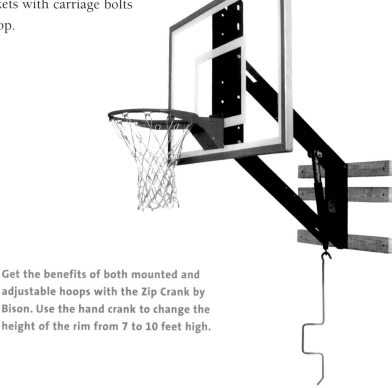

Get the benefits of both mounted and adjustable hoops with the Zip Crank by Bison. Use the hand crank to change the height of the rim from 7 to 10 feet high.

GO-O-O-AL!

HOST YOUR OWN WORLD CUP WITH
AGE-APPROPRIATE EQUIPMENT

A soccer ball and a stretch of lawn may be all young children need to get
their kicks. But for older kids who want more serious practice, set up a
mini-field with a portable goal or two and some accessories. Few yards have
the room for a full-size regulation field, which can measure as large as 100
by 50 yards, but a reduced version is even better because it allows players
more touches and shots on goal.

Goals made for home use are typically easy to move or can be stored
to make room for other activities. They are often made of galvanized steel
or aluminum with nylon netting. Newer types made of plastic (such as
PVC) can fold up or have removable netting, allowing even easier storage.
Another option is a rebounding soccer goal, which is good for practice and
takes up minimal space.

Regardless of size and materials, even small portable goals must be
anchored firmly in place to prevent tipping. Depending on the product, you
can secure the goal in the ground with an anchor or with stakes, pegs, or
some type of counterweight. Heavier goals require stakes or pegs that you

ABOVE: **All you need is
a ball to convert a lawn
into a soccer pitch.**

hammer into the ground. Follow the manufacturer's instructions carefully, making sure to anchor the goals fully each time you move them.

To make play even more realistic, use flags or cones to define a mini-field. With a tape measure and marking chalk or aerosol paint (found at sporting goods stores or online), measure and mark the midfield line (at the halfway point along the length of the field), center circle, and goal areas.

LEFT: There's no shortage of portable soccer goals for backyard use. You can find ones in a wide range of sizes, materials, and even colors.

BELOW: Flexible mini-goals like this one make setup and removal very easy when it's time to mow the lawn or switch to a different sport.

Perfect Pitch

The size of youth league fields varies widely, and your backyard field dimensions will depend on yard space as well as kids' ages. The American Youth Soccer Organization recommends the following maximum dimensions, which you can use as a guide:

AGE	FIELD DIMENSIONS	GOAL AREA	GOAL HEIGHT	GOAL WIDTH	BALL SIZE
Under 6	30 by 15 yards	*	4 feet	2 yards	3
Under 8	50 by 25 yards	6 by 12 yards	6 feet	6 yards	3
Under 10	80 by 40 yards	6 by 15 yards	7 feet	7 yards	4
Under 12	100 by 50 yards	6 by 20 yards	8 feet	8 yards	4
* no official recommendation for this age group					

HOME-FIELD ADVANTAGE

OUR GREAT NATIONAL PASTIME HAS NEVER GONE OUT OF FASHION WITH KIDS. But you don't have to go to the local park to hear the crack of a bat. To lay out a mini-baseball field, complete with pitcher's mound, all you need is an open, level area of ground, some basic tools, and baseball equipment. If you build it together, the kids are guaranteed to come! An alternative for families with limited space is a portable pitcher's mound that you can store when you need the yard for other activities.

A baseball diamond is basically a 90-foot square. For Little League, it's considerably smaller at 60 by 60 feet; Pony League is midsize at 75 by 75 feet. Use the dimensions in the chart below to plan a full-blown home field, or just to set the distance from the rubber to the plate to hone your child's pitching arm.

In the yard, a pitcher's mound and home plate are all you need to create a practice area for pitching and catching.

Build It

To construct a realistic field, or even just a section of a diamond for practice, gather the following tools: a shovel, two 200-foot tape measures, a sledge-hammer, several bags of clay and sand, a tamp, stakes, bases, the pitching rubber, home plate, and marking chalk. A roller for creating the slope of the pitcher's mound and aerosol paint for marking base paths are optional.

Create an outline or footprint of your field so you can visualize it before committing yourself. Designate any elevated areas of ground as infield. Start with home plate, which determines the rest

Diamond Dimensions

FIELD SIZE	HOME TO SECOND/ FIRST TO THIRD	PITCHING RUBBER TO HOME	BASE TO BASE	HEIGHT OF PITCHING MOUND
Little League	84 feet, 10$\frac{1}{4}$ inches	46 feet	60 feet	6 inches
Pony League	106 feet, $\frac{3}{4}$ inches	54 feet	75 feet	8 inches
The Majors	127 feet, 3$\frac{3}{8}$ inches	60 feet, 6 inches	90 feet	10 inches

of the field. Check your sight lines and make sure you have a barrier (such as a fence or shrubs) for containing stray balls.

From the back tip of home plate, measure the distance to second base (see chart). Mark this point with a stake. This will be the center of second base. Again, measuring from the back tip of home plate, mark the pitching rubber.

Use two tape measures to locate first and third bases. Stretch one piece of tape from the second base stake toward the first base area; stretch the second tape measure from the back tip of home plate. Where the two tape measures cross at the 60-foot mark is the back corner of first base. Repeat for third base.

To create the pitcher's mound, measure a circle 12 feet in diameter. The pitcher's rubber (which is 18 by 5 inches) will rest at the top of the mound. The height of the mound ranges from 6 to 10 inches. The mound should be built from the ground up, with a slope beginning 8 inches in front of the rubber and descending 1 inch for every foot toward home plate. Tamp (or roll) as you add layers of soil. The ideal mound material is made of 40 percent clay, 40 percent sand, and 20 percent silt.

Lay out your bases. Around home plate, which is 17 by 8½ by 12 inches, use chalk or paint to draw a circle 18 feet in diameter. Create two 3-by-6-foot batter's boxes—for righties and lefties—next to home plate. Batter up!

Buy It

Several companies sell portable pitching mounds built to regulation standards. They come in different sizes to match various baseball levels. Though some models can be folded up and rolled away, most require two people to carry them and set them up. You can move the smaller mounds out of the way when you need to, as well as fit them in a car or truck for trips to the park.

The backyard is the perfect place for honing skills between games.

Glove Care

To make your baseball or softball glove last, take your time breaking it in. Don't overdo application of the oil or foam designed to soften the leather—too much could actually damage it. Don't spit in the glove, which will also harm the leather. Instead, apply the amount of conditioning product suggested on the label, work it into the palm area, and remove any excess with a paper towel.

Create a pocket for catching balls by placing a ball in the mitt, closing the glove around the ball, and tying a string or wrapping a rubber band around the entire glove. Put it aside for a day or two. An even better way to mold the glove is to use it.

Protect your glove by never leaving it outside where heat and rain could deteriorate it. If it does get wet, wipe it dry with a towel and let it air-dry indoors. To maintain the inner lining, consider using a batting glove underneath to absorb sweat (unless you're a pitcher).

GET A JUMP ON FUN

FEW ACTIVITIES ARE MORE EXHILARATING THAN SOARING UP IN THE AIR ABOVE A TRAMPOLINE. You and your spouse will probably find the trampoline irresistible as well, and an enjoyable way to get exercise.

Bouncing gently or high in the sky challenges the body in various ways, testing balance, coordination, and agility. It's also great for just clowning around.

Backyard trampolines have increased in popularity in recent years, but they've also gotten a bad rap because of a rise in trampoline-related injuries. By buying high-quality products and following safety suggestions (see Safety Tips), you can make trampoline play safer. For example, trampolines that are built over a pit with the mat at ground level eliminate the risk of falls from an elevated surface. Another safety feature that comes with newer aboveground models is netting to prevent jumpers from falling off the sides. With spring-free trampolines, you don't have to worry about kids landing on hard springs.

ABOVE: **Use your trampoline to practice and train for other sports, including diving, gymnastics, and snowboarding.**
BELOW: **This spring-free model allows kids to leap with confidence by providing a safety net on all sides and eliminating the risk of jumping on springs.**

Trampoline Features

Before selecting a trampoline, explore the many different varieties online or at sporting goods stores. Here are a few factors to weigh:

● SIZE AND SHAPE. Trampolines come in various shapes, such as squares, circles, and rectangles. For young children, or in a tight yard space, a small round model, sometimes referred to as a rebounder or jogger, will provide plenty of excitement. A somewhat larger junior trampoline, either a circle measuring 6 feet in diameter or a 4-by-8-foot rectangle, is more typical. Older kids, teens, and adults will get more bounce out of a trampoline if it has a diameter of 14 feet or an equivalent rectangular size. Check the manufacturer's guidelines for age recommendations.

● WEIGHT RATING. Tramps come with weight ratings measured in hundreds of pounds. Consider the weight of the heaviest person who will be using the trampoline (see Safety Tips), as well as the warranties for the mat and springs.

- INGROUND AND ABOVEGROUND. While it's easier to install an aboveground trampoline on top of grass, an in-ground one built over a pit may be safer. If you go with an elevated tramp and have small kids, choose one that sits 1 to 2 feet high. Trampolines designed for older kids and adults are set higher.

To install an in-ground trampoline, you'll need to dig a pit and install a drain for water. For safety, it's still recommended that you surround the pit with an enclosure or shock-absorbent material such as wood chips to a distance of 6 feet in all directions.

Materials

Trampolines are typically constructed with galvanized steel frames, tempered springs, and a mat. The frame's strength is key to stability and durability; the heavier the gauge, the better. It should not bend, flex, or bow.

Jumping mats or beds are usually made of strong polypropylene or nylon material that creates a solid, webbed, or string surface. Webbed or string beds offer the best bounce. Look for ones with UV-resistant material and thick polyethylene foam padding over the springs, hooks, and frame—a child could get injured by falling on exposed pieces. Mesh netting to enclose the tramp is a wise investment. Ask the manufacturer about using an anchor kit, with augers and buckles, to secure the trampoline in the ground. And a cover will protect it from the elements.

Accessories

To add to the fun, look for basketball hoops, balls, bounce boards, bungee cords, ladders, tents, and other extras made especially for trampolines.

Safety Tips

Most trampoline injuries occur at home to children under age 15. For safe play, keep these guidelines in mind:

- Position the trampoline far from other structures, trees, and power lines in the yard. Place it on top of a soft, level landing surface (not concrete). There should be 5 to 6 feet of clear space on all sides.
- Cover the springs, hooks, and frame with thick foam padding.
- Supervise kids whenever they use the trampoline. Teach them to jump in the middle, where they are less likely to fall off the edge of an unenclosed tramp. Beginners and small kids should avoid risky stunts like flips or somersaults. More adventurous jumpers should have a spotter on hand.
- Allow only one person to jump at a time.
- Don't allow children under 6 to use a full-size trampoline.
- Check that all parts are correctly connected, secured, and in good condition.
- Use a trampoline enclosure. There are also safety nets that enclose the bottom of some tramps to prevent a child or pet from going underneath while others are jumping on top.

CHILDREN DON'T
NEED MUCH MORE
THAN SAND TO HAVE
A GOOD TIME. FOLLOW
THE TIPS ON THE FOLLOWING
PAGES TO SELECT THE BEST SPOT
FOR SAND PLAY AND BUY SAFE
MATERIALS.

sand play

THE SCOOP ON SAND

AS PLAY ELEMENTS, SAND AND WATER ARE GOLD MINES. Kids love to feel the squish of sand between their toes. They like to dig and scoop and let the grains fall through their fingers. Add water, and children can mold or sculpt sand into just about anything. With these simple ingredients, they create all sorts of inventive activities.

Water also holds special appeal in its own right. Kids are fascinated by the interplay of light on water, by objects that float on it, by drips and splashes.

To contain the mess, carefully consider the placement of sandboxes and water sources. Since sand brushes off easily when it dries, you can reduce the amount of sand that winds up in your house or on patios by locating a sandbox some distance away from those areas. A gravel path or lawn creates a good transition. Another option is to install an outdoor shower or simply attach a hose to a faucet for cleaning off.

Also think about the direction and angle of the sun. Sandboxes should be shaded or children won't be able to play in them for hours on end, but a total absence of sunshine isn't a good idea either. Ultraviolet rays help keep the sand dry and sanitary. The best compromise may be a setup that allows both sun and shade, particularly in the summer.

TOP: **A flat space of some type is as crucial in a sandbox as a countertop is in a kitchen.**

BOTTOM: **A used tire makes a compact yet full-service sandbox.**

What Makes a Great Sandbox?

- ADEQUATE SIZE AND DEPTH. The ideal size for a sandbox is roughly 4 by 8 feet, but kids can enjoy plenty of play with a smaller version. Ideally, the sand should be about 12 inches deep so kids won't hit dirt or concrete when they dig.
- BORDERS. Sandboxes need a rim to contain the sand and prevent it from blowing into other parts of the yard. Install an earthen berm or a wood, stone, or concrete border. Leave the bottom of the box unenclosed, however, so water can drain out.
- FLAT SURFACE. Provide a level plane for making sand pies or as a launching pad for toy helicopters. Locate this within the sandbox, rather than along an edge, to keep sand inside. If you do opt for a flat rim, try to place the overhang on the outside; if it must be on the inside, check often for spiders, which love dark spaces. The ledge should be strong enough to support the weight of an adult who may want to join children in their play.

Selecting Sand

The best sand for play contains clean, rounded grains of the same small size. This type is better for packing and sculpting because it is less likely to become compacted or hard when wet. There is no official standard for sandbox sand, so one supplier's play sand may be quite different from another's.

Garden rocks and a stone path create natural borders for this unboxed sandbox.

If technical data is available, ask for sand with a grain size between 30 and 50, and a silt and clay content below 5 percent.

Sand is far less expensive by the truckload than by the bag, but to get it delivered you may need to buy several cubic yards. Bags, however, are easier to handle and install yourself. For a 4-by-8-foot box 12 inches deep, you'll need 32 cubic yards of sand.

Safe sand. Most commercial sand contains extremely fine shards of crystalline silica because it comes from quarried quartz rock. Silica dust has been linked to serious lung disease and cancer among construction workers who are exposed to large amounts day after day. A child's exposure to the carcinogen is far less than that of construction workers, but you can take steps to minimize the risk.

- Buy play sand, which tends to have grains of uniform size, rather than all-purpose sand.
- Encourage children to make the sand damp so it doesn't generate dust.
- Consider buying sand that doesn't contain crystalline silica. Feldspar, for example, is a safe mineral.

Play sand

All-purpose sand

Silica-free sand

Uninvited Guests

To keep cats and other animals out of the sandbox, always use a cover when kids aren't playing. Some sandboxes come with their own fitted hard covers, or you can install a mesh or tarp cover cut to fit the box. Look in a garden store for plastic or vinyl netting intended to deter deer or birds. It comes in pieces big enough to cover even the largest sandbox; order an additional 3 inches of material to overhang all sides. To hold the mesh in place, slip it over metal hooks or cup holders (curved end pointed down) screwed to the outside of the sandbox. You can also order fitted covers that come with screws and steel snaps.

A GALLERY OF SANDBOXES

TODDLERS THROUGH ELEMENTARY SCHOOL—AGE KIDS will get hours of play out of sandboxes. There are many ways to foster years of sand play in the yard. Don't settle for just any design: Consider different approaches for combining sandboxes with other structures and elements. Experiment with everything from placement to borders to create a special spot for sand adventures.

LEFT: **Neatly tucked within a play set, this sandbox is shaded by a slide and two climbing walls. To keep uninvited guests away at night, protect the box with a fitted mesh or tarp cover. On the far side of the sandbox, a 2 × 4 discourages children from venturing into the swing area, where a collision could occur.**

BELOW: **Blend a sandbox into the surrounding trees and flowers by using rocks as borders instead of wood. While rocks keep sand from escaping, they also present a hazard if kids trip and fall on them. Be sure to supervise play and show young kids how to get in and out of the sandbox to prevent mishaps.**

ABOVE: This large sandbox is also the landing pit for a wide slide. The slide's gentle slope keeps kids from coming down too fast, while 2 × 6s on the top edge of the sandbox keep sand and toys inside.

LEFT: Just look at what you can fit in this 14-by-14-foot sandbox. Framed by rustic cedar logs, it accommodates serious sand scooping toys and multiple kids.

SAILING ON SANDY SEAS

KIDS CAN GET THEIR HANDS DIRTY
BUILDING COUNTLESS CREATIONS
IN THIS CLEVER SANDBOX THAT YOU
CAN BUILD IN A WEEKEND

This nautical-themed sandbox includes a hidden base that allows sand to be twice as deep as the boat is high. The all-weather fabric sail provides shade, and the seats serve as platforms for castles and other creations.

In most construction projects, builders begin with the foundation and then build the structure on top. For this project, it makes more sense to work in the opposite order. First, build the boat; next, the foundation. Then, excavate and, with a helper, move the pieces into place.

Building the sandbox is almost as easy as assembling a simple box, except for a few special cuts. To give the sandbox its boat shape, the side pieces need to be cut at a 45-degree angle. That requires beveling the edges of the end pieces at a 45-degree angle so the shelves can sit flat. No special joinery is required; screws or bolts hold everything together. Add a bell and a captain's wheel, and bid "Bon voyage!" as children sail off to magical lands.

Sewing the Sail

The sail was made from outdoor-rated polyester upholstery fabric, but all-weather acrylic fabric will also work well. Hem the edges and ends, using a double overlap of about 1/4 inch on the sides and 2 inches on the ends. Insert a large grommet at each corner, following the instructions on the package.

This junior sailor can play for hours in his shaded sandbox.

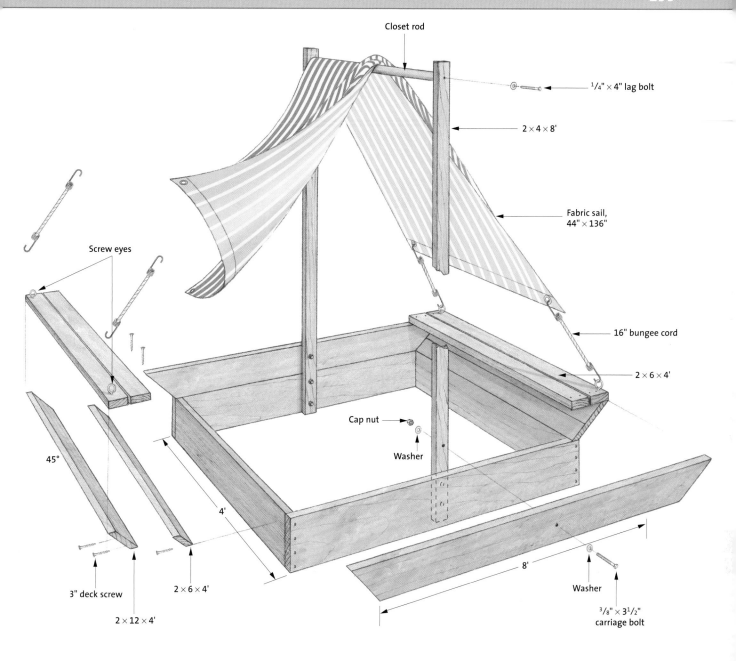

Closet rod

$^{1}/_{4}$" × 4" lag bolt

$2 \times 4 \times 8'$

Fabric sail,
44" × 136"

Screw eyes

16" bungee cord

$2 \times 6 \times 4'$

45°

Cap nut

Washer

4'

8'

Washer

3" deck screw

$2 \times 6 \times 4'$

$2 \times 12 \times 4'$

$^{3}/_{8}$" × 3$^{1}/_{2}$"
carriage bolt

Materials List

- Six $2 \times 12 \times 8'$ planks pressure-treated wood
- Three $2 \times 6 \times 8'$ planks pressure-treated wood
- One $2 \times 4 \times 8'$ piece pressure-treated wood
- Closet rod, 1$^{1}/_{4}$" × 4'
- Two $^{1}/_{4}$" × 4" lag bolts
- Two $^{1}/_{4}$" cut washers
- Four $^{1}/_{2}$" × 1$^{1}/_{2}$" screw eyes
- Four 16" bungee cords

- Six $^{3}/_{8}$" × 3$^{1}/_{2}$" carriage bolts with 12 washers
  and 6 cap nuts
- Box of 3" galvanized deck screws
- Four yards 45"-wide outdoor fabric
- Roll of thread
- Four large grommets
- Two cubic yards sand
- Wood glue

Building Instructions

1 **BEVEL THE SIDES.** Because the sandbox sides are cut at a 45-degree angle, the top and bottom edges of the end pieces must be beveled at the same angle. Use a table saw, a jigsaw, a hand plane, or, as shown here, a circular saw. Adjust the saw's guide to a 45-degree angle, then make the cut.

2 **BUILD THE HULL.** Assemble the boat upside down on a flat surface so that the top edges align. With deck screws, attach the end pieces to the sides. Fill the gap on each end with a 2 × 4, beveled to match the other end pieces. For added strength, apply a strong wood glue to joints before securing with screws.

3 **MEASURE THE FOUNDATION.** Using the upside-down boat as a guide, mark the 2 × 12s that will become the boat's foundation. The side pieces should equal the length of the boat at its base. Cut the side pieces to fit (the foundation requires only straight cuts), and secure foundation boards to each other with deck screws.

4 **DIG YOURSELF A HOLE.** Mark the sandbox perimeter with spray paint. Then dig out an area slightly larger than the exterior of the foundation box. The depth should equal the width of a 2 × 12—about $11\frac{1}{2}$ inches.

5 **PLACE THE BOAT ON THE FOUNDATION.** With a helper, move the foundation box into the hole and check the sides to make sure they are level. Shim with small rocks if necessary. Then set the boat on top. Add a few angled deck screws to tack the pieces together.

6 **PREPARE THE MASTS.** In each 2 × 4, drill a $\frac{1}{4}$-inch hole $1\frac{1}{2}$ inches down from the top. At the other end, drill three $\frac{3}{8}$-inch holes. Locate them 4, $15\frac{1}{2}$, and 19 inches from the bottom.

7 **RAISE THE MASTS.** After bolting the masts to the boat frame so they are plumb, cut the closet rod to fit the distance between the tops of the masts. Attach the rod by clamping a scrap of wood to one mast while you secure the other end of the rod with a lag bolt.

8 **SECURE THE BENCHES.** Space the bench boards about $\frac{1}{2}$ inch apart and fasten with deck screws. Then insert one screw eye at each corner. For added torque, use the shaft of a screwdriver to tighten.

9 **ADD SOME SAND.** Fill the boat with sand, stopping about 4 inches from the top.

10 **SET SAIL.** Spread the fabric over the closet rod and attach to the screw eyes with bungee cords. If there's too much slack, adjust the tension by knotting the cords.

JUST ADD WATER

A NEARBY WATER SOURCE ADDS A WHOLE NEW DIMENSION TO SAND PLAY. HERE'S A WAY TO GET AN OUTDOOR FAUCET WITHOUT HAVING TO CALL A PLUMBER

Materials List

- Foam-lined hose of sufficient length
- Backflow preventer, if needed
- Pressure-treated post, 4' or 5' long
- Gravel or concrete mix to fill hole around post
- Two ½" pipe clamps, with screws
- Hose-to-pipe adapter
- Teflon tape (to wrap pipe threads before assembly)
- Three ½" 90° galvanized pipe elbows, each with one internal and one external thread
- Threaded galvanized pipe, ½" × 24" long
- Self-closing shower valve (available from plumbing-supply stores)
- River rocks, a grate, gravel, or bark to protect faucet area from becoming muddy

When Candace and Erik Jagel tore into their yard for a basement waterproofing system and a new septic field, their boys wasted no time discovering the play value of a sand pile trucked in by the construction crew. So as the yard went back together, the family included an oversize sandbox in their landscaping.

With heavy equipment already on hand to do the hard work, the family sculpted the slope in front of the house to create a nest for a circular sandbox 12 feet in diameter. Because the digging was effortless, they made the sand a generous 3 feet deep. The sand is set directly into the earth, and a rim of masonry blocks defines the perimeter.

The family shares a well with several neighbors. Fearing that the boys might overtax the supply, the parents at first had a rule against using a hose in the sandbox. The lure of water with sand proved irresistible, however. An underground water line equipped with a self-closing shower valve solved the problem. Now Sean, 7, and Lucas, 9, pull a chain or lower a handle and water gushes out—but only as long as they hold the tap open.

Installing a Flexible Water Source

Extending permanent outdoor plumbing can be a big project if it requires digging a trench several feet deep. A far easier method is to bury a hose a few inches deep. If you use a type lined with foam (see Resources), it won't burst from freezing water. The foam compresses to accommodate the expansion as ice forms.

Connect the hose to a faucet that is designed to keep the water from being siphoned back into the drinking-water supply if pressure drops. Outdoor faucets installed within the past decade should have this health-protection feature. Older faucets can be retrofitted by adding a fitting called a backflow preventer. Note that most modern outdoor faucets drain to eliminate the danger of ice, but not if hoses are connected. Unscrew the sandbox water line as winter approaches.

House water supply

Backflow preventer

Post

Shower valve

Elbow

Pipe clamp screwed to post

½" × 24" pipe

Elbow

Hose to pipe adapter

Coil and bury excess hose. Don't cut it and splice on a new connector.

RIGHT: **There is no trench to dig in this easy method for extending a water line. Align a flat spade next to the hose and slice straight down into the soil about 4 to 6 inches. Rock the spade back and forth to create an opening in which the hose will fit. Soil that's too compacted needs to be loosened first with a few quick jabs of a pick. Without removing the spade, stuff the hose as deep as possible into the opening. Then push the dirt back into place and move on to the next section.**

FAR RIGHT: **Sean fills a bucket easily from a self-closing valve designed primarily for showers.**

INVENTOR'S SANDBOX

GIVE KIDS SOME SAND AND WATER, ADD A FEW WHEELS AND INCLINED PLANES, AND THEN LET THE EXPERIMENTATION BEGIN

This sandbox features a play board with numerous attachment points. The board rises 3 feet across the back of the sandbox, allowing enough room for devices to be arranged in a way that one action triggers another and then another. The inclined planes, for example, can be set up to channel sand into the wheel, which in turn will dump sand into the box with the trapdoor. These various configurations keep these kids busy for hours.

The play board devices bolt into a network of T nuts that are inserted from the back. Use bolts that are long enough to thread through the T nuts and project far enough beyond to hold a lock washer and a standard nut, so they won't come loose. Snug the bolts up against the T nuts when you fasten things to the play board.

Where very young children are at play, parents should tighten the bolts because washers are small enough to be a choking hazard. For older kids, omit the extra nut and lock washer and provide a wrench so that they can loosen and move the parts themselves. Designing and adding new features is half the fun.

The sandbox itself is simple and quick to build. It consists of four layers of 4 × 4s topped by a 2 × 6 rim. This construction allows for the 1-foot-deep sand to sit a few inches below the rim so less sand spills out of the sandbox during serious play. Because this sandbox is located next to a pine tree, it was not possible to dig out soil beneath the box. On other sites, excavating would allow deeper sand or shorter walls.

Deep sand and wall-mounted physics keep these preschoolers busy for hours. Give older kids the materials and tools to create their own configurations.

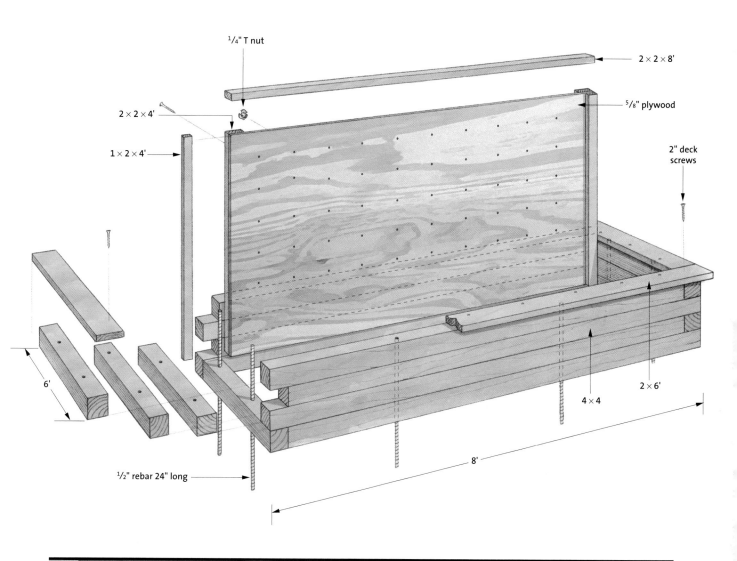

¼" T nut

2 × 2 × 8'

2 × 2 × 4'

⅝" plywood

1 × 2 × 4'

2" deck screws

6'

2 × 6'

4 × 4

½" rebar 24" long

8'

Materials List

SANDBOX

- Eight pieces 4 × 4 × 8', four pieces 4 × 4 × 12' *

RIM

- Two pieces 2 × 6 × 6', one piece 2 × 6 × 8' *

PLAY BOARD

- One 2 × 4 × 8' cut in half *
- Trim: one piece 1 × 2 × 8', one piece 2 × 2 × 8'

OTHER MATERIALS

- Rebar: eight pieces ½" × 24"
- One box 2" deck screws
- One 4 × 8' piece ⅝" exterior plywood
- Forty ¼" T nuts
- Forty-eight cubic feet sand (approximately 1¾ cubic yards)
- Waterproof glue
- Clear packing tape

*use pressure-treated wood

Building Instructions

1 **BUILD THE SANDBOX.** After stacking the 4 × 4 posts so their ends overlap in opposite directions, use an extra-long bit to drill two ¹/₂-inch holes through all layers of each side. Then pound rebar through the holes until the metal is flush with the top of the wood. A 2 × 6 rim screwed onto the tops of the 4 × 4s will hide the exposed rebar tips.

2 **ATTACH THE PLAY BOARD.** Smear waterproof glue on the outside of the T nuts and hammer them into place from the back. They must go in straight and seat fully so the prongs lock into the wood. Then screw the plywood to the 2 × 4 supports at both ends of the sandbox. Leave a 1¹/₂-inch gap on both sides for 1 × 2 trim pieces. A trim piece across the top covers the remaining exposed edge of the plywood.

Outfitting the Play Board

Equip the board with ready-made items as well as devices you build at home. When interest in one piece of equipment wanes, replace it with something fresh. Encourage kids to dream up their own gear.

A. This funnel, sold for changing car oil, comes with tubing attached. An alternative would be a standard funnel, a length of tube, and a hose clamp or piece of duct tape to hold the parts together.

B. Two plastic cups suspended from a bar of wood that pivots create an adjustable scale. To keep each cup upright, an eyebolt extends through a hole in the bottom. A nut and washer on each side of the plastic hold the bolt in place. Instead of a single pivot point, there are several holes in the bar, so kids can reposition the bar and learn what it means to have a relative center of gravity.

A

B

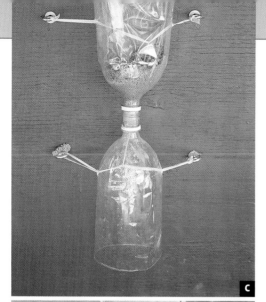

C. Two plastic soda bottles taped together provide a see-through double funnel when the ends of both bottles are removed. If you use the same concept but leave the end on one bottle, the contraption becomes an hourglass.

D. A simple box made of 1 × 4 pine provides hours of fun thanks to the trapdoor at the bottom. Pivoting on a hinge, the door stays shut thanks to a magnetic cabinet latch. But when kids pour enough sand into the box, the weight overwhelms the magnet and the door pops open, sending the sand cascading out.

E. A shelf gives kids a handy place to store sand toys, plastic teacups, or decorations for sand art projects. Building the shelf is very easy. Take a length of 1 × 3 pine for the shelf, and nail, screw, or glue it to a same-length piece of 1 × 1, which will provide support from underneath. Drill $5/16$-inch holes into the 1 × 1 for the mounting bolts, and the shelf is ready to install into the play board. Paint before mounting, if desired.

F. Reminiscent of the Chutes and Ladders board game, these simple inclined planes channel sand down the board. Kids can also tie a cup and a toy car to opposite ends of a short string and see how much sand needs to be poured into the cup to pull the vehicle uphill. The ramps are lengths of 1-inch corner molding.

   Below the ramps is a red sand spinner. Modeled after a water wheel, it has four compartments made of two rectangles of 1 × 3 pine cut to interlock. The wheel is $1/4$-inch plywood in a $6^1/2$-inch-diameter circle. The mounting bolt fits into a $3/16$-inch hole drilled through the center. Washers on both ends allow the wheel to spin freely. As sand pours in, the wheel begins to rotate and eventually spills its load.

RESOURCES

PAGES 4–5
All-Safe Pool Safety Barriers
800-786-8110
www.allsafepool.com

PAGES 12–13
Trex Co.
800-289-8739
www.trex.com

Oasis
800-962-6973
www.alcoa.com

PAGES 16–17
Ear Protection:
Peltor Kid
peltorkid.co.uk

Child Safety Glasses:
Dyno-Mites
manufactured by
Sellstrom Manufacturing
800-323-7402
www.sellstrom.com

Supplier:
Enviro Safety Products
800-637-6606
www.envirosafetyproducts.com

PAGES 18–19
"Handbook for Public
Playground Safety"
Consumer Product
Safety Commission
800-638-2772
www.cpsc.gov

Measurements of children at
different ages can be found on
the AnthroKids database at the
National Institute of Standards
and Technology,
ovrt.nist.gov/projects/anthrokids.

PAGES 24–25
Louise Hassan
The Children's Garden Company
415-454-1121
www.childrensgardenco.com

PAGES 28–29
All-Safe Pool Safety Barriers
(see above for contact
information)

Cover-Pools Inc.
800-477-2724
www.coverpools.com

PAGES 32–33
Practical Folly Playhouses
905-658-0915
www.practicalfolly.com

La Petite Maison Playhouses
877-404-1184
www.lapetitemaison.com

PAGES 38–39
Building Materials Reuse
Association
800-990-2672
www.buildingreuse.org

PAGES 42–49
HomePlace Structures
866-768-8465
www.homeplacestructures.com

PAGES 54–55
Pacific Play Tents
877-722-0083
www.pacificplaytents.com

PAGES 56–61
Basement Water-channel Liner:
Platon
800-265-7622
www.systemplaton.com

PAGES 66–67
Thompson's WaterSeal
800-367-6297
www.thompsonswaterseal.com

PAGES 70–79
TreeHouse Workshop, Inc.
206-782-0208
www.treehouseworkshop.com

Malleable Iron (or Round)
Washers:
Tacoma Screw Products, Inc.
800-562-8192
www.tacomascrew.com

Heavy-duty Exterior
"Star Drive" Screws:
Screw Products, Inc.
877-844-8880
www.screw-products.com

PAGES 82–83
Rubber Mulch:
Close The Loop
866-629-8414
www.closetheloop.com

Rubber Flooring Products:
Diamond Safety Concepts
800-842-2914
www.diamond-safety.com

PAGES 84–85
Swing Set Mall
866-297-PLAY
www.SwingSetMall.com

PAGES 86–87
Barbara Butler Artist-Builder, Inc.
415-864-6840
www.barbarabutler.com

PAGES 88–89
Rainbow Play Systems
800-724-6269
www.rainbowplay.com

PAGES 92–93
Swing Set Mall
(see above for contact
information)

Bouncy Swing:
Spring Swings, Inc.
561-845-6966
www.springswings.com

Hammock Swing:
Rainbow Play Systems
(see above for contact
information)

PAGES 98–103
Swing-N-Slide
800-888-1232
www.swing-n-slide.com

PAGES 104–105
Heavy-duty Trolley and
Installation Parts:
Outdoor Fun Store
877-386-1700
www.outdoorfunstore.com

Lighter-weight Trolley:
Fun Ride Deluxe, made by:
Spring Swings
(see above for contact
information)

PAGES 110–111
Backyard Sports Center
800-268-3586
www.backyardsportscenter.com

PAGES 112–115
More Information about
"North Shore" Freeriding:
604-833-6796
www.nsmb.com

PAGES 116–117
SunRamp Solutions
877-978-6726
www.sunramp.com

MojoRails
480-829-0412
www.MojoRails.com

Plans for Other Styles of
Skateboard Ramps:
"Thrasher Presents How to Build
Skateboard Ramps," edited by
Kevin Thatcher; High Speed
Productions, 2001.

PAGES 118–119
Zip Crank by Bison
800-247-7668
bisoninc.com

PAGES 120–121
American Youth Soccer
Organization
800-872-2976
www.soccer.org

PAGES 120–121
"Baseball Field Layout and
Construction"
Baseball Almanac
www.baseball-almanac.com

Outdoor Fun Store
(see above for contact
information)

PAGES 122–123
International Trampoline
Industry Association
541-984-0332
www.itia-inc.org

"Trampolines at Home, School
and Recreation Centers"
American Academy of Pediatrics
847-434-4000
aappolicy.aappublications.org

PAGES 124–125
Springfree Trampoline
866-899-7370
www.springfreetrampoline.com

PAGES 128–129
Silica-free Sand:
The Safe Sand Company
415-971-1776
www.SafeSand.com

PAGES 136–137
Foam-lined Hose (6-ply, ⅝-inch):
Flexogen
Manufactured by Gilmour Group
800-458-0107
www.gilmour.com

Self-closing Shower Valve:
Chicago Specialties #350
Manufactured by
Dearborn Brass
800-321-9532
www.dearbornbrass.com